BURNOUT SUCKS!

How to be wildly creative and live to enjoy it!

JIM HOUGH

nts!
nurture the spark!
PUBLISHING

Published in Evansville, Indiana, by NTS! Publishing.

Library of Congress Cataloging-in-Publications Data

Hough, James A.
Burnout Sucks! How to be wildly creative and live to enjoy it! / Jim Hough

ISBN 978-0-9964938-0-2 (Paperback)

2015910001
Printed in the United States of America

For my children: Emily, Christy, Brad, and Becca.
You have taught me more about enjoying life than anyone else.

I love you bigger than the sky.

CONTENTS

1. A Good Place to Start

"Burnout is not a condition that gets better by being ignored."
Herbert J. Freudenberger

A Culture of Burnout

We live in a culture of burnout. We're encouraged to work hard and play hard. We criticize the workaholic out of one side of our mouths and applaud their dedication and commitment to excellence out of the other. We're told that we can have it all—an incredibly successful career and a happy, fulfilling family life. We smile and lift our imaginary glasses in mock toast saying "Live life to the fullest because there will be plenty of time to sleep when we're dead!"

There's an old saying in the advertising business, "If you don't come in on Saturday, don't bother coming to work on Sunday." It's that kind of thinking that is burning us out and killing our ability to create. We are driven by the misconception that the more hours we work, the more productive, prolific, and prosperous we will become. But here's the rub: that thinking was discredited over 100 years ago!

In the early 1900s, the Ford Motor Company ran all kinds of tests to find the best ratio of hours worked to productive output. After dozens of scenarios, they found that the right number of hours worked to produce the best return is 40 hours a week. Adding 20 hours initially increased productivity slightly, but that increase reversed itself in less than a month, and productivity slid downhill. Ford officially adopted the 40-hour workweek in 1926.[1]

How Much Are You Willing To Give?

A close friend of mine is a senior executive for a large Midwestern power company. He once said to me, "Our company will take as much of an employee as he or she is willing to give." He wasn't trying to sound flippant or cruel. He was just stating a fact. The company you work for is not really looking out for your best interest. Companies are in business to make money. There's only one person who has a vested interest in making sure you stay healthy and productive: you.

We must ask ourselves just how much we are willing to give. What are the tradeoffs? What is the real return from investing 50, 60, or more hours a week in our work? Is it worth it?

"To harness the courage we need to get on the right path, it pays to reflect on how short life really is and what we want to accomplish in the little time we have left." [2]
Greg McKeown, *Essentialism*

A Good Place to Start

There's always more money to make, more things to buy, more tasks to perform. The one thing there isn't more of is time. We get 24 hours a day. That's it. As James Taylor sings it, "Time may be money, but your money buys no more time."[3] Time is not a renewable asset. Once spent it is gone forever.

As you hold this book in your hands, you are standing at a crossroads. You, like so many others who make a living by creating, are facing a decision. Will you continue down the road of exhaustion and burnout, or will you make a commitment to change? I'd like to suggest a good place to start. Find the nearest cemetery, and take a walk. I know it sounds a little morose…but bear with me. Go take a walk and think about all the lives represented by the various headstones. Think about all the goals and dreams left unfulfilled, all the "things" left undone. Not all the money in the world can add a single hour to any of these lives.

But you still have time. No matter how old or young you are, you have time. Pause right now, grab hold of your unique, creative potential; make a commitment to do whatever it takes to nurture it, protect it, and enjoy it. Every one of us has something to contribute to the world, but you are the only one who can ensure that your contribution will make its way into reality.

THE ROAD AHEAD

In the following pages, I will tell you the story of my own burnout and things I've learned through the trials and errors of finding my way back. It starts as a sad story. I'm betting it will be a familiar story to many of you. The good news is that it doesn't end as a sad story. There is hope and encouragement. There is a practical, real-life system to follow that will help you integrate proven, healthy principles of living and creating into your life.

Here's my promise to you: If you will walk through this stuff with me and apply even a few of the principles we talk about, you'll feel that spark of creative potential stir. The more you apply, the brighter it will shine. The subtitle of this book includes the phrase "wildly creative." I didn't overstate things. There is a way for all of us to be wildly creative and live long, healthy, creative, satisfying lives of contribution.

Promise.

WHAT DOES BURNOUT LOOK LIKE?

2. WHAT DOES BURNOUT LOOK LIKE?

"We see the world, not as it is, but as we are"
Stephen Covey

WHAT IS IT?

The long-awaited field trip was finally here. Mr. DeAngelo and his 6th-grade class were on the bus and ready to go. The kids were studying zoology and what better place to do that than at the zoo? Upon their arrival a zookeeper escorted the group into a large room. Mr. De Angelo said, "Class, before we start our tour of the animal kingdom, we're going to have a test." Groans floated up from the group. Mr. DeAngelo continued, "We're going to give each of you a blindfold to put on. The zookeeper will then bring in something special. When it's in place, we will guide each of you close to it so you can reach out and touch it. Take your time, and see if you can tell what it is just by feel."

So, each of the kids put on a blindfold, and a large metal door slid open. They heard the sounds of shuffling and scraping as though several people were working hard to move something heavy across the floor. Then, the large door was pulled closed.

The students were each led to a different spot where they could reach out and touch the object. There was some giggling and squirming, but in a few minutes, everyone had had a turn. Then, the door was opened again, the workers hauled the object back through the door, and the class was allowed to remove their blindfolds.

"Well, what do you think it was?" asked Mr. DeAngelo.

One student raised his hand and said, "It was a rope. A tough, old rope that was frayed at the end."

Another said, "No, it wasn't. It was a tree. It was a big tree with rough bark. I couldn't reach around it, even with both my arms."

Someone else said, "What are you talking about? It wasn't rough at all. It was smooth and long and a little pointed at the end, like a huge sword or something."

Yet another said, "It was a big snake! Kind of narrow at one end, but thicker the farther up I reached."

The discussion went on like that for several minutes, with each student convinced of what he or she had touched.

Mr. DeAngelo said, "Now, kids, be reasonable. How can all of you be right?"

The great metal door screeched open again, and in came the zookeeper, leading a great bull elephant. It shuffled across the floor, making little grunting noises as it walked. In an instant, they all knew it was true. They were all right...they had just touched a different part of the elephant; some the tail, some the leg, others the tusk or trunk.

Burnout Defined

Does that little story sound familiar? It's a new take on the old proverb about six blind men and an elephant.[1] It originated in India many centuries ago, but the truth it conveys is just as relevant today as it was in its first telling. Our experiences in life are determined by our own perspective and situation.

Burnout is defined by Dictionary.com as:

1. A fire that is totally destructive of something.
2. Fatigue, frustration, or apathy resulting from prolonged stress, overwork, or intense activity.

Both definitions have merit. Just like the kids reaching out to touch a different part of the elephant, we each have our own perspective on burnout and how it has impacted or might impact us. It's a matter of situation, perspective, and degree. We often think that the way we experience the world is the way everyone experiences the world. After talking with lots of creatives from lots of different disciplines in lots of different places in their careers, I realized that my experience was just one among many. Burnout comes in many different sizes, shapes, and colors. The one thing we all agree on is…it sucks!

Sometimes the easiest way to discover something about ourselves is to see it in the life of someone else. What follows is a potpourri of personal descriptions of burnout shared by creatives just like you and me.[2] See if any of these personal, varied, and unique comments ring true for you.

> *"What is most personal, is most universal."*
> Carl R. Rogers

WHAT IS MOST PERSONAL

"The word 'burnout' sounds so final. So hopeless. But I think that a creative professional starts to wilt like a morning glory bloom at noon when the end product of his labors no longer resembles anything he truly cares about. Or when he is no longer doing work that requires or incites the creative neurons of the brain to fire."

"Burnout happens when your work becomes routine. I despise the phrase 'it is what it is.' On the other hand, I am a proponent of the proposition 'If it ain't broke, break it.' When you become convinced that something is routine and anyone can do what you're doing, the inevitable question is, 'Why should I be doing this?' And nothing can cause burnout faster than that."

"Unable to perform the necessary tasks to complete a project. Tired. Dog tired. Depression may occur. Looking at a 'blank canvas' and it remains blank. For. a. very. long. time."

"Being unable to produce what is expected of you or what you expect of yourself creatively."

"Burnout is when a rouge voice in my head says, 'That's good enough,' I know at this point there are too many external forces attacking me, and I am looking for a place to hunker down. "

--

"I have always associated it with burning the candle at both ends, trying to accommodate everyone in your life all at the same time without any help."

--

"I mean, after 10 years of doing Valentine's Day promotions... how many ways can you say, 'It's Valentine's Day. Order flowers now!' So, then, you feel you've lost your creative touch and think, I can't do this anymore."

--

"Maybe it means that you come to a place where you just can't have another creative, original way of doing the same thing."

--
"With passion for our craft comes pride. The fear of rejection or a negative reaction can break down our confidence and the ability to think creatively. Sometimes it seems we'll never hit the mark, and self-doubt settles in."

———

"Burnout happens when there is no end in sight, no rest from the pressure of coming up with ideas and the pressure to keep doing something over and over until it is 'perfect' (which never happens)."

———

"Mostly, I think it means you just can't bring yourself to put your stinking boots on and go into the office."

———

"Letting routine suck the life out of you. Routine is needed, but there needs to be variety in routine."

———

"The amount of creative 'energy/fuel' that comes into me is exceeded by the amount of creative 'energy/fuel' that comes out of me. I get burnout when I'm creatively exhausted and haven't had enough opportunities to feed myself creatively."

Did You Catch a Reflection?

Do any of the quotes sound familiar? If so, you're not alone. There are as many definitions for burnout as there are people experiencing it. Each is unique, and yet somehow familiar. Much of what we perceive to be personal pain and struggle is actually part of the universal experience. That's why programs like Alcoholics Anonymous and others like it have been so successful over the years. It's not that misery loves company but that hurting people find strength and hope amidst common suffering. Once we realize that we are not alone in our pain, it becomes easier to believe that together, we can find a way through the darkness and back to creating again.

In the next chapter, I will tell you the story of what burnout looked like in my life. I bet it will sound familiar.

WHAT DOES BURNOUT LOOK LIKE?

3. Down In Flames

"There are wounds that never show on the body that are deeper
and more hurtful than anything that bleeds."
Laurell K. Hamilton, *Mistral's Kiss*

I have worked in advertising and marketing as a creative professional for more than 30 years. I know what it means to be creative in a create-on-demand[1] culture. I know the stress of constant deadlines and ever-increasing client demands. What once took weeks to produce can now be done in hours…and it's expected to be done in hours. Fewer hours than ever before. Somehow I managed to survive the first 25 years of my career. But on October 7, 2007, I burned out—and it almost killed me.

Crossing the Line

It was one of those weekends at the office trying to finish up a presentation I would give early the next week. I couldn't get our technology to work—computer crashes, printer jams, email down. I was alone in the building. Without realizing it, I started talking to myself. Loudly. In fact, I began swearing and yelling at the top of my lungs every time something went wrong. Restarting my laptop, fishing out a paper jam from the printer, I started going ballistic. Spewing strings of expletives, slamming doors, kicking trash cans.

Then, without warning, a line was crossed. Rage, like some self-loathing demon, seemed to invade me—to possess me. I felt as though I was being dragged about against my will, punching at the air, screaming at equipment, losing my grip. Then I felt a searing flash of pain. It happened so fast that I didn't realize what had happened until I was bent over, holding my head, stunned. I had slammed my forehead into a brick wall. It left a mark—and a massive headache. I nearly passed out.

It scared me.

Finally, after several more painful hours, I had finished up. But, the damage had been done.

Breaking Point

On the way home, I remembered just one little thing that I'd forgotten. I snapped. I began screaming at the windshield, banging my hand on the steering wheel. I felt as if I had stepped outside myself. I became unaware that the noise, the shouting, and tears were coming from me. It all became a blurry background of foggy, confusing white noise. I felt a desperation that was like nothing I'd ever experienced. It was dark, hopeless—there was no air. I was suffocating. I became aware of the median: 20 feet of grass between me and the semi barreling west toward me. One flick of my wrist, and it would finally be over. I could finally be done. I could finally get some rest and relief. There was so much yelling and screaming. So much rage, so much hurt, so much disappointment…then, nothing.

I don't remember slowing down. I don't remember taking the exit. I have no idea how I ended up in an empty parking lot. But, there I was, sobbing into my hands.

Eventually I made my way home and went to bed. Somewhere in the night of October 7, 2007, it happened—not with yelling and screaming, but with quiet resignation. I was through. I didn't have anything left, no inner resources, no spark of creativity, nothing. I wrote my wife and my boss an email during the night. It was a rant about all that was wrong with my life. It was a rambling explanation about how I had gotten to this dark place. It was, in some ways, a suicide note…I just didn't have the energy to follow through with it.

I was broken.

On Monday morning, October 8, 2007, my dear wife found me on the living room floor. By the end of the day, I had voluntarily checked into the locked ward of a psychiatric hospital. This was, I thought, how it was going to end for me.

4. 8 Days, 8 Weeks, 8 Months

"Man cannot remake himself without suffering,
for he is both the marble and the sculptor."
Alexis Carrel

8 Days

If you've never been admitted to a psychiatric hospital, let me tell you, it's an interesting experience. By definition, you have to be in "crisis" in order to qualify for admittance. It was the fear that I would hurt myself that ultimately led to the decision to be admitted. So, in the midst of the this dark and hopeless place in my life, I had to give up all my worldly possessions, my clothes, my shoes (because of the laces), my belt, and anything else that could be fashioned into a weapon. I then, for the first time in my life, experienced a full-body cavity search. Apparently, you can hide dangerous things in there. After that, I was allowed to go to my room and sleep.

The next morning I was awakened by a nurse and told to take my meds. I learned that the first step in treatment is to quell the crisis. I was already on some meds for depression, high cholesterol and type-2 diabetes (other consequences of living a life out of balance). So, the meds were just an increased dosage of one and a new, short-term, fast-acting "wonder drug" intended to back me away from the ledge and calm me down. Within hours I was more relaxed and, though still in a hopeless fog, feeling less like doing anything stupid.

As life in the ward began to stir, I sat on the edge of my bed in a daze. The day before seemed like a distant memory from another lifetime. It played over and over in my mind, almost as though I needed the repetition to convince myself that it had really happened. As I sat there, my vision beginning to clear, I became aware of something. There wasn't a sharp corner or hard edge anywhere around me. Everything was rounded, padded, or in some way softened. Every precaution had been taken to create a safe environment where I could not hurt myself even if I wanted to.

Before even realizing what I was doing, I had begun to think, But if I were going to kill myself…how could I do it? Something inside had flickered just a bit. There was absolutely no way to hang anything anywhere. The idea of fashioning the sheets into a makeshift noose was out. The sharpest things within reach were my fingernails, which are always cut short. In the end I decided my only option would be to try and swallow the odd little rubber-soled "footie" socks I was issued to keep my feet warm. That sounded like entirely too much work.

LIFE IN THE JOINT

I was taken on a short tour of the place, which basically consisted of a long hallway of patient rooms and the lounge where you could sit and read, watch "approved" TV, and talk with other inmates. There was more to the facility, but it was on the other side of a locked door. A locked door. That was the first time it hit me: I'm not in Kansas anymore. I was staring at a locked door, and I didn't have the key. I wasn't in control anymore. The realization brought about an odd combination of relief and fear.

There were 10-12 others "in-house" with me. That number fluctuated daily, depending on discharges and admittances. These people weren't in straight jackets. There was no drool dripping down their chins. They looked lost, dazed, and broken. There was one young lady who just cried and rocked herself for the first couple days. And one guy, who would occasionally, stand and spin in circles. For the most part though, they all looked like, well, they looked like me. I didn't know any of them, yet I felt strangely at home. There's an unexplainable connection between suffering people, even if the pain and circumstances are very different.

My first evening and day were mostly relaxed and I was left to do whatever I wanted. On day 2, things changed. There was a schedule. We ate meals at a specific time. We had group therapy at a specific time. We did activities at a specific time. Rebuilding structure and routine into life was the first important coping skill we were taught. We were given free time in between the structure, but it was simply part of the routine. Looking back, I recognize that this gave me a sense of normalcy: I do this first, then that.

As part of that routine, I would talk to the resident psychiatrist each day. At our first meeting, I knew that he and I would get along well. In his office was a bookcase filled with superhero action figures: Superman, Spider Man, even Underdog. Each day's visit was short and predictable. He asked me a series of questions that helped him to determine where I was on the path to recovery. This evaluation was one tool they used to determine my length of stay. He'd ask me things like, "On a scale from one to ten, how sad do you feel? Do you want to hurt yourself? On a scale from one to ten, how angry do you feel?" One question in particular struck me as funny. "Are you hearing any voices?" (Aside: One day I had a different psychiatrist meet with me. She was a little more formal than my superhero doc. When we got to the "Are you hearing any voices?" question, I answered, "Well, none that I don't recognize." She slowly looked up at me over her glasses and said calmly, "We don't joke about the voices." That struck me as even *more* funny, but I kept my mouth shut.)

Taking Action, Any Action, Helps

Beyond the locked door was a carpeted gymnasium (I kid you not), the cafeteria, and a couple rooms for small groups to gather. One had art supplies in it—the activity room. During daily activity time, we would work on simple projects like collages and posters related to feelings or coping skills we were learning about. We would play volleyball in the gym (which is a very different game when all the players are depressed and medicated). Everything was geared toward helping us to act, move, and think differently. It was as though we were all trapped inside some hard-shelled cocoon, and all the activities were intended to chip away at it—a crack here, a small divot there, a process of freeing us from some self-made prison. Initially that felt very annoying. All I wanted was be left alone in that cocoon. But, these young, enthusiastic therapists were trained to overlook my resistance and keep me moving, talking, and playing.

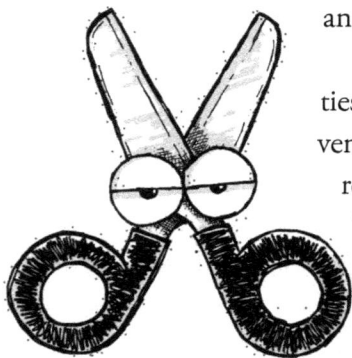

To be honest, I didn't enjoy the activities, not even a little bit. They seemed juvenile and pointless. But, in hindsight, I realize that having fun was not the point. The point was to keep me moving—to keep me engaged in something, anything, other than just sitting by myself in the corner sucking my thumb. I mean, there was a consistent theme of coping skills education, but I wasn't really paying attention. In an odd, distant sort of way, just being engaged, moving my body, cutting out pictures from magazines (with those round-tipped safety scissors, of course) and slapping the volleyball made me feel a little better. Lighter, somehow.

TOGETHER IS BETTER THAN ALONE

The group therapy was an interesting experience. We were encouraged to talk about ourselves—our feelings, our struggles, our fears. In the beginning we were like billiard balls, just bouncing off each other—not connecting in any meaningful way. But, over the course of a few days, people began to open up more and more. I was struck at just how broken some of these poor people were. I had much more to hope in than many of them. I had a wife and four kids that loved me. I had an older brother who had gone through a similar experience and was very supportive. My dad had called to tell me he was praying for me and loved me. I had a boss who supported me not only emotionally, but also financially throughout my entire ordeal. Some of these people didn't have a single person in their lives they could point to and say, "There, that person loves me." The therapists were very clear about how everyone's pain is relative…but I was gaining some perspective about the nature of suffering nonetheless.

Over the course of my eight days there, I did connect with several people in a meaningful way. We didn't share any personal information that would identify us outside the joint—no last names, no places of employment, no specifics. But, that made it even easier to talk candidly about what hurt. Though many friends and family could provide sympathy for what I was going through, these people, these broken people gave me empathy. They understood my pain in a way that outsiders could not. Without even knowing my full name, where I lived, or what I did for a living, they knew me. They were like me. That was a powerful connection.

The Spark

Around day five I felt something different. I became a little less content to sit in front of the television during free time. (The limited channel selection played a role in that, I'm sure.) I wanted to do something. My wife had brought me a sketchbook on the second day, hoping that I might want or need it. The staff wouldn't give it to me in the beginning. It had a hard cover, with sharp corners—no telling what havoc I could stir up with a weapon like that. Moreover, by definition, I would need a pen or pencil to do anything with that hardcover WMD. Eventually, though, after persistent requests, the superhero doc gave the attendants permission to give it to me.

It surprised me just how precious that book and pen felt in my hands. In a way, it was like being given a little piece of my "normal" life back. I found an out-of-the-way place just to be alone with my thoughts (though I was never out of sight of the staff. "Alone" wasn't a good thing in this world). What I felt was an urge to express myself. When I was admitted, I was empty. I was certain that the spark had gone out—crushed, drowned, and buried. But, even in the midst of my hurt and darkness, I felt the urge to write and to draw. The feel of the pen moving across the semi-rough paper was healing, familiar, right.

In those remaining days inside, and then nearly every day afterward, I wrote about my hurt. I wrote about my life. I drew cartoons about the oddity of living in the "coo-coo's nest." I began ingesting the coping skill concepts I'd been taught. I realized that things had to change. I had to change.

8 WEEKS

After what seemed like both an eternity and the blink of an eye, I was discharged. Eight days had been enough to get me through the crisis and on to the next step. As I mentioned before, when someone is suicidal, the first order of business is to subdue the crisis with medication, rest, and very close monitoring. Once you've been backed off the ledge, step two is the gentle infusing of structure, routine, and education. After a time, you're then released back to your own life in a limited way. I was able to go home, but I was to attend group therapy every day, Monday-Friday for five hours a day.

The rules were the same as before: no personal information. Confidentiality was central to the success of our time together. The group varied from 10-15 people each day, men and women, young and old, people from a variety of economic, cultural, and situational places. Like inpatient care, the makeup of the group changed nearly everyday, but there was still a sense of connectedness and unity.

A team of three to four therapists took us through the day's activities—each with her own unique personality and way of conducting the group. The variety was helpful. One, in particular, was especially helpful to me. Her name was Linda (changed to protect privacy). She was old, wrinkly, and tough. She was not what you would picture as the ideal therapist, but she was perfect for me. Whenever I would share, she would challenge me if she thought I was being less than genuine. She would not let me get away with just saying what I thought the group, or she, wanted to hear. In the end, she really challenged me to dig deep and make the most of this opportunity.

THE DIRTY LITTLE SECRET

After a full Eight weeks, in my final session with the group, I thanked everyone for their help and insights. I felt ready to re-engage with my life. I was nervous and scared, but ready. After the little ceremony we had for each person who "graduated" back to his or her life, Linda took me aside. She looked me straight in the eye and said, "I have a dirty little secret to tell you. There isn't a doctor, a pill, or other person in the world that can make you get and stay healthy. We're all here to help you. But, the only person that is going to make you take your life back and live it is you." It felt like a punch to the gut at first. What was I supposed to do with that? How could she put that kind of pressure on me, just as I was starting to feel my sea legs? How could my only hope of getting my life back be me? I was broken. I was hurt. I was, well, I was just me. To her credit, in spite of the tears welling up in my eyes, Linda didn't try to soften the tone of her statement. She didn't hug me and tell me, "There, there, everything is going to be okay." Instead, she slapped me on the shoulder and said, "Don't screw it up."

Linda was exactly the therapist I needed.

8 MONTHS

The same week that the outpatient program ended, I began seeing a private therapist. His name was Phil. He was a gentle soul, who helped me give some context to what I had learned and how not to screw it up. We worked on the coping skills and how to use them to move forward in recovery. We worked on setting up real-istic routines: morning routines, bedtime routines, even routines at work.

During those eight months of weekly therapy, I began to realize just how reckless I had been with my life. It's easy to set yourself up for burnout when you're young. Youth masks a lot of the wreckage that results from pushing too hard. We bounce back quickly from all-nighters, poor nutrition, and sitting for hours on end in front of a computer screen. But, the effect is cumulative. For me, it was my 40th birthday. "Suddenly" I had knee problems, high cholesterol, and type 2-diabetes, only it wasn't sudden at all. The damage had been building gradually and finally reached a tipping point.

5. The BeHABITS!

*"To become what we are capable of becoming
is the only end in life."*
Alexis Carrel

A Story of Two Creative Lives

Somewhere in the not-too-distant past, there were these two guys. Recently graduated from their respective universities, they were ready to jump into the workforce and begin their careers in advertising. Both had considerable creative talent and were looking forward to making their own contributions to the industry.

Match was dynamic, outgoing, and very talented. He began his career in a flash of creativity. One project after another was met with amazing insight and thought-provoking solutions. He worked long hours and never complained. His work gained immediate recognition, and his name spread throughout the advertising world as an up-and-comer!

Candle, on the other hand, began more gradually. He, too, was talented and excited about making his mark. He listened, learned, and became more and more confident in his own abilities. Each new assignment was an opportunity to improve his skills and provide more valuable input. His work began to get noticed, and he found himself on a slow but steady rise in success and satisfaction.

Very Different Paths

As the years went by, both Match and Candle became well-known for their creativity and contributions. But, the paths they took looked very different. Match found it harder and harder to maintain a balance between his life and his work. He often could

not separate the two. The rapid pace and intense pressure of his lifestyle began to take a toll. He experienced periods of sleeplessness and depression due to stress. He couldn't imagine getting through the day without a constant steam of coffee, energy drinks, and cigarettes. And, he had to change antidepressants several times just to approach a sense of normalcy.

Candle was no stranger to stress or pressing deadlines. When long hours were required, he would work them. But, he had also built important routines into his life. He made time for rest and refreshment. He turned down many opportunities to get involved in worthwhile activities, not because he didn't want to participate, but because he knew his limits. Candle valued his creative talent more than recognition. He valued his ability to contribute consistently, over the long haul, more than trying to please everyone. He knew that his relationships—family, friends and co-workers—grew more and more precious as time passed.

The Results

In the end, Match burned out. The quality of his work declined. His ability to contribute dried up. Eventually, no one remembered his name. Candle continued to contribute at a high level. His work increased in quality and importance. He mentored many others who also went on to make valuable contributions. His life was fulfilling, and many counted themselves blessed for having known and worked with him.

Does either of these stories sound familiar? Does one sound more familiar?

Be First, Then Do

Referring to the power of "being," James Autry, in his book *The Servant Leader* says, "This is not a trick or a gimmick. This isn't a technique. It's not even a process. It is a conscious choice about how you choose to be and about how you choose to live your life…"[1] Autry is making the point that one can't do the right things if one does not first decide to be the person who can do the right things. Match never had a chance to find the right balance of life and work. Why? Because he chose to be a match, and matches, by definition, burn out. It didn't occur to him that he could be anything else.

He was wrong.

The Value of Habits

Habits are funny things. They can be good for us, or bad. Habits can give us the structure and discipline we need to be productive, or they can bind us like iron shackles that hinder our growth. Habits come in all shapes and sizes, from the order we do things in the shower (seriously, take note of that today) to the path we follow through the grocery store. Good, bad or indifferent, habits are part of the human experience.

66 Days. Really?

66 Days—according to a 2009 investigation[2], that's about how long it takes, on average, to have a new behavior become automatic—meaning that a person starts performing the behavior without much conscious thought. I'd always heard that it only takes 21 days. 21 days sounds a lot more doable than 66 days. The truth is, it's different for everyone. Some of us are wired to adapt to new routines and habits easily, while others are a little more resistant to change. I fall into the latter group—the 66ers. In his book *The Early To Rise Experience*, Andy Traub says, "The only number that matters in building a habit is 1. Habits happen 1 decision at a time."[3] Regardless of how long it takes to form a new habit, it's going to require some effort.

What the Heck is a beHABIT?

In the previous chapter, I told you the story of my own experience with burnout and eventual recovery. Those eight days, eight weeks and eight months led me to organize the new information I was given into eight principles that would help me remember and apply those learnings. I call them the beHABITS! Each starts with "be" to emphasize the importance of making the conscious choice to beCOME the person, who can then do the things that will keep us on a path away from burnout and toward a life of unique, wildly creative contribution.

beHABITS! are much less about things we do and much more about people we want to become. Some habits are easier to integrate into life—like taking out the trash on Monday nights, or paying the mortgage on the 15th of the month. Habits like those are all about doing something specific at a specific time. beHABITS! are different. beHABITS! encourage us to make fundamental changes in the way we interact with the world and the people around us. beHABITS! encourage us to become different than we are now. So, the term beHABIT! is a tool to help us remember that the things we'll be learning on our journey together are much more than things we will do. These new habits will help us to "beCOME" something new.

NOTHING NEW UNDER THE SUN

In the Bible, King Solomon said "What has been will be again, what has been done will be done again; there is nothing new under the sun."[4] The truth of this statement has played out time and time again in my life and work. Most ideas are the result of other, older ideas rearranged and re-imagined. So it is with the beHABITS! I didn't invent these concepts. I just compiled them together in a list so they might be easier to remember and implement.

THE BEHABITS!

beLIEVE!
beBRAVE!
beCURIOUS!
bePLAYFUL!
bePRESENT!
beCONNECTED!
beRENEWED!
beGRATEFUL!

Let's walk through each one and see if we can find a path that leads to your wildly creative, happy, healthy life of contribution.

THE BEHABITS

be LIEVE!

**BELIEVE THAT WE ALL HAVE A UNIQUE,
CREATIVE CONTRIBUTION TO MAKE IN THE WORLD.**

6. BELIEVE!

*"The stronger our beliefs become, the more
powerfully they drive our thoughts and actions.
Our behavior will reflect what we believe."*
Henry Marsh, *The Breakthrough Factor*

JUST A PAINTING

In July of 1888, an artist put the finishing touches on a painting depicting an arid landscape of twisting oak trees, bramble, and sky. He wasn't very happy with it and decided just to give it to his brother. (Give it to family. They'll take anything.) It surfaced again in 1901, when it was sold to a French art dealer. It sold again in 1908 to an aspiring collector. To his dismay, the painting was declared a fake, and the young collector banished it to the attic where it sat in the dark, collecting dust for nearly seven decades. When the man passed away in 1970, the painting was rediscovered, only to be declared a fake for a second time. Again, it slipped back into obscurity.

Twenty one years later, someone found the painting and asked a prominent art museum to examine it. The museum declined. A decade after that, the museum reconsidered and agreed to look at the painting. In 2011, armed with a new collection of letters from the artist, the experts reached the consensus that the painting was a lost work of acclaimed painter Vincent van Gogh. Van Gogh mentioned the painting in three letters and identified it by the number 180, which he had written on the back. Chemical and X-ray testing were done, and the conclusion was undeniable.

Roughly 37 by 29-inches, Sunset at Montmajour is now

prominently displayed at the van Gogh Museum in Amsterdam, which receives more than a million visitors a year.

What's It Worth?

What is it that determines whether a painting is tossed into the attic or displayed in an exclusive gallery for millions to see? Answer: the value placed on the painting. When Sunset at Montmajour was thought to be a fake, everyone believed it was worthless and treated it accordingly. But, once it was discovered to be a genuine artistic treasure, everything changed. It was carefully cleaned, examined, and transported to a climate-controlled environment where it would be protected and preserved.

As creative professionals, we have the ability to look at the world from a unique perspective. We're able to see beyond what's visible and envision unseen possibilities. The blank notebook becomes a novel. The quiet becomes a melody. The sketches on a napkin become a Sunset at Montmajour.

What is that worth to us?

Do we believe this ability we share to be just a tool—an implement that, once used up, gets tossed into the attic? Or do we see it as a gift, a treasure, something of true worth to be shared with the world? The answer determines how we treat it.

beLIEVE! calls us to reevaluate what we believe about our ability to create—our spark of creative potential—and why it's been given to us.

Got Purpose?

The Purpose Driven Life, written by Rick Warren, was published in 2002. The book has been on the New York Times Best Seller list for advice books for one of the longest periods in history! It's been at the top of the Wall Street Journal and Publishers Weekly charts and has sold over 32 million copies in over 85 languages. Everyone we live with, work with, play with, shop with, cry with, and laugh with—all of us—are desperate to believe we have a purpose in life. We are desperate to believe we have a contribution to make, a unique, creative contribution that only we can make.

Those of us who create for a living find it easier to make the connection between our gift and our purpose. About seventy percent of the creatives I've interviewed or surveyed see their ability to create as a gift and believe that they have a unique, creative contribution to make to the world. That's the good news. But, we still have to answer the question: what is that worth to us?

Whether we ever consciously answer that question or not, what we believe becomes clearer with each passing year. The more in tune with our gift and purpose we are, the more carefully we will nurture and protect it. Once the energy of our youth begins to wane and the reality of having to take better care of ourselves becomes more obvious, things change. We change. We make decisions that guard our creative potential. We say no to projects and schedules that demand more of us than we can give. We look for balance in life that will feed our ability to create rather than starve it. Why? Because we believe that our ability to create is something special—a treasure—and we need it in order to make our own unique, creative contributions to the world.

However, if we believe our creative potential is nothing

special, life begins to look very different. The energy of youth leaves earlier…maybe even in our mid-to-late 20s. Our health begins to unravel at the edges. Anxiety and stress become common bedfellows. Sleep becomes difficult and erratic. Our attitude and outlook on life lean more toward half-empty.

Yet, here's the irony: in the midst of our deterioration, we may be producing the best work of our lives! We might be winning awards and getting all kinds of attention from peers and clients. We destroy our ability to create and contribute over the long haul in exchange for a fleeting act of brilliance and recognition. We become flesh and blood examples of Aesop's fable of The Goose and the Golden Egg. The fable of a farmer who has a magic goose that lays golden eggs—one at a time. In a fit of impatience the farmer kills the goose to get at the precious treasure all at once. But when he opens the goose, it's empty. He only succeeds in killing the possibility of receiving any golden eggs in the future.

It's a Wonderful Life

The 1946 holiday classic *It's a Wonderful Life*[1] tells the story of George Bailey, a small-town banker who sees his life as so desperate that he contemplates suicide. From a young age, his dream had always been to leave Bedford Falls and travel the world, but circumstances got in the way. He gave up his own education so his brother could go. He kept the family-run savings and loan afloat after the death of his father. He protected the town from the greedy banker, Mr. Potter. He married his childhood sweetheart, but that isn't enough. As he prepares to jump from a bridge, his guardian angel, Clarence, intercedes and shows him a vision of what life would have become for the residents of Bedford Falls if he had never been born.

In that vision, George sees that, out of all the residents of Bedford Falls, he and he alone has been the driving force behind keeping his little town safe from the dark-hearted Mr. Potter. His compassionate heart, deeply held values, and business sense are what ultimately lead his fellow citizens out of the clutches of Potter and into the promised land of the American dream—family, home, and the pursuit of happiness.

George Bailey had a particular set of skills and a purpose. His life mattered—not just to him, but to his family and many, many others in his world. Once that became clear to him, things changed. He changed.

BELIEVE!

We won't make the right decisions concerning our talents and purpose until we beCOME the kind of people who can make those decisions. Working harder, pushing ourselves to the edge over and over, squeezing the life out of the golden goose for one more brilliant idea… these will not make us more creative. They will burn us out.

beLIEVE! that you have been given the gift of creative potential and that there are unique, creative contributions that you and you alone can make. This is where being wildly creative and living to enjoy it begins.

BE BRAVE IN THE FACE OF FEAR AND DOUBT.

7. BE BRAVE!

"To live a creative life, we must lose our fear of being wrong."
Joseph Chilton

Fear Is Universal

We're all afraid of something. Fear is also very personal; things that scare me don't necessarily scare you. Fear comes in all shapes and sizes, and every one of them is a creativity killer. Probably the most famous quote about fear comes from our 32nd president, Franklin D. Roosevelt: "The only thing we have to fear is fear itself."[1] He said it during his first inaugural address in 1932. The Great Depression was at its worst, and he knew that the people needed hope. They needed to believe that, as a nation, we could overcome our difficulties. Those ten words have been most quoted and beloved of the speech, but the rest of that sentence is significant as well: "nameless, unreasoning, unjustified terror which paralyzes needed efforts to convert retreat into advance."

One significant fact about fear is that it can't hurt us. It doesn't have any teeth. It's an emotion and nothing more. Whenever my children would tell me they were afraid of something (like standing up in front of class or asking a store clerk for help), I would encourage them with, "Don't worry, they can't eat you." And with a roll of their eyes and a smirk, they would find the courage to press on. It's a goofy thing to say, but it's also true.

Nameless, Unreasoning, Unjustified Terror

FDR really hit on something there. Our fears are usually nameless, unreasoning, and unjustified. When we embrace these nameless, unreasoning, unjustified fears, they paralyze us. They stop us in our tracks and prevent us from making the "needed efforts to convert retreat into advance." President Roosevelt was pleading with a nation to face down fear and, together with our fellow citizens, begin doing the work required to overcome.

This very same principle applies to cultivating and protecting our unique creative potential. This isn't about pretending that fear isn't real, it's real all right. It's about embracing the fact that this nameless, unreasoning, unjustified terror can't eat you.

"Courage is not the absence of fear but the judgment that something else is more important than fear. The brave may not live forever but the cautious do not live at all. For now you are traveling the road between who you think you are and who you can be."
Meg Cabot

WHAT IS FEAR?

If we're going to face and overcome fear, we should understand what it is to begin with. Here's a definition: "An anxious feeling, caused by our anticipation of some imagined event or experience." This concise definition comes from Karl Albrecht, Ph.D., in his column "BrainSnacks"[2] (love that title!) for Psychology Today magazine.

In this article Dr. Albrecht states "When we let go of our notion of fear as the welling up of evil forces within us...and begin to see fear and its companion emotions as basically information, we can think about them consciously. And the more clearly and calmly we can articulate the origins of the fear, the less our fears frighten us and control us."

Fear is just information. And it's information about something that hasn't happened yet! Seth Godin says it this way: "Anxiety is experiencing failure in advance."[3] He adds that worry sucks as a way of preparing ourselves for what's to come.

WHAT DO WE REALLY FEAR?

In my own life and career, I have had to deal with three specific fears more than any others:

- Fear of being wrong
- Fear of what others think
- Fear of being exposed

When I was in college, I had a graphic design professor who gave us a little speech on the first day of class. It started with, "For every design challenge there is only one best solution." He repeated the statement and then told us he expected us to commit ourselves to finding that one best solution. From where I sit today, some 35 years into my career as a creative professional, I can see that he was trying to inspire us. He was trying to motivate us to work hard and not settle for the first idea that came to mind. But, as a student on the first day of class…I was mortified! Every single kid in that class was mortified.

Walking back from class, I thought What if the solution I come up with is…wrong? What if, after investing hours and hours on this first assignment I end up bringing the wrong solution to class? And if I am wrong, then what will everyone else think? I'll be exposed for the non-artist I really am."

Don't you just love school? On that first day of class, I experienced all three of my worst fears—all at the same time.

Obstacles: Sources of Strength

In the wonderful little book, Art & Fear, David Bayles and Ted Orland help us to see that "our flaws and weaknesses, while often obstacles to our getting work done, are a source of strength as well."[4] Our fears are often two sides of the same coin. On the one side is the obvious risk of being wrong, the risk of failure. But, the other side is the opportunity to grow. Take the common metaphor of a butterfly in a cocoon. That cocoon is both an obstacle and an opportunity. If the butterfly only worries about the obstacle that stands in the way of its freedom, it dies a prisoner. However, if the butterfly chooses instead to pursue freedom, in spite of the obstacle, it gains strength in the process of overcoming. And, having overcome, it now can fly!

Being Wrong

Human beings like things to be predictable. We like to imagine the ideal circumstances in which we think we could be the most creative. That thinking is one of the biggest hurdles to overcome. In our longing for things to be perfect before we actually start creating, we inadvertently give life to the fear that things won't be perfect and, therefore, we won't be creative, or that we'll do it wrong because things weren't perfect. Bayles and Orland go on to tell us that what's really needed is "an overriding willingness to embrace mistakes and surprises along the way."

Being wrong is part of being creative. You really can't make any kind of creative contribution without doing it wrong a few times. There's just no other way to do it.

"Surprises and reverses can serve as an incentive for great accomplishment. I have not failed. I've just found 10,000 ways that won't work."
Thomas Edison

In our insistence that we do everything right, we miss the very opportunity to move closer to our greatest contribution. Had Thomas Edison seen "doing it wrong" as a sign that he should quit all this nonsense, you'd be reading this by candlelight. That design teacher I told you about was partly right. It's not that there is only one right solution, it's that there are many wrong solutions along the path to a right solution. And, the really fun part is that the solution you end up with may not be the one you thought you were going to end up with!

Mistakes and surprises are two sides of the same coin. You can't have one without the other. Being wrong is not a bad thing. It's a needed thing. It's a stepping stone to the place we want to go, a constant companion on the journey to our unique, creative contribution. Being wrong can't eat you.

What Are They Thinking?

Humans are obsessed by what we think others are thinking about us: how we look, what we drive, the quality of our work, and on and on. Psychologist Dr. James Dobson, founder of Focus on the Family, said, "We are not who we think we are. We are not even who others think we are. We are who we think others think we are."[5] It is possible to waste literally years of our lives worrying about what we think others are thinking about us. This endless speculation kills the creative spark from the inside out, and we're the ones who give it that kind of power over us.

In part, I blame this on the media—advertising specifically. We are bombarded with messages telling us that we are judged as people by the shape of our bodies, the clothes we wear, the neighborhoods we live in, the watches on our wrists, the cars we drive, the brand of soda we drink, and even the antidepressants we take. We're still trying to keep up with the Joneses.

If someone were to ask us, "Do you believe that the kind of shoes you wear determines your innate worth?" We'd be quick to say, "Of course not!" Yet for years we didn't wear white after Labor Day. Even in a country like the United States—the birthplace of independence and individualism—we still long to fit in. Isn't that what's really at the root of all this? We just want to be part of the "in" crowd, accepted, even admired. Those desires are totally human. Everyone is created with the need to be understood and accepted. The problem comes when those natural desires grow into such powerful emotional needs that they threaten our very lives like the loss of oxygen would. When this happens, the natural response of self-preservation kicks in. We start to perceive even the possibility of criticism as a life-threatening event.

We're afraid that what others think can eat us.

Remember, as Dr. Albrecht said earlier in this chapter, we need to consider fear as just information. Then, and only then, can we think clearly and calmly about how to respond to it.

Remember the old nursery rhyme "Sticks and stones may break my bones, but words will never hurt me"? It's only partially true. Words can hurt us—a lot—but only if we let them. The criticism of others can sting if we take it too much to heart, and there will always be critics. There is no superpower to make everyone "like" us. Wanting to be liked is normal. Needing to be liked is dangerous. We can avoid this danger by receiving all criticism as simply information. Can it help us improve our work, our attitude, our life, or not? Beyond helpful suggestions that others may pass along, there is no value to criticism. We don't have to be afraid of it. As we form the habit of beBRAVE!, we will begin to see criticism in a new way—toothless!

> *"At age 20, we worry about what others think of us. At 40, we don't care what they think of us. At 60, we discover they haven't been thinking about us at all."*
> Jock Falkson

I just love that quote. I categorize it as one of the undeniable truths of life: People just aren't thinking about us as much as we think they are. We've all got busy, complicated lives to live. Our own thoughts are occupied with an incredible amount of details about family, work, friends, money…you name it. The thoughts of others are just as occupied with their own stuff. It may be a blow to our ego, but in the end, it's a relief to realize that most people don't spend any more time thinking about us than we do about them.

If They Only Knew the Truth About Me

I got the first big break in my career when an acquaintance at church saw some graphic design work I had done and asked me if I'd be interested in applying for a job opening at the company where he worked. Little did I know that conversation would eventually lead me to living in a different part of the country—for the rest of my life! (Funny how things happen that way!) I went from working in the art department of a small retail chain of drugstores to working in a global, multibillion-dollar corporation in a matter of weeks. My salary and responsibilities more than doubled overnight. Driving home after my first day on the job, I wept uncontrollably—not out of gratitude for this incredible opportunity—but for fear that they would soon discover I was not capable of doing the job and fire me! Had it not been for my dear wife (and cheerleader), I might have thrown myself off a bridge somewhere. Over time, I grew into that new position and earned the trust and respect of my coworkers.

I shared this experience with an old high school friend not too long after it had happened. He laughed out loud and admitted that he, too, found himself in a similar situation from time to time. He worked for Kodak as a meeting facilitator. His job was to help keep the people around the table on task and reach a productive outcome. Occasionally, he would do this for a group of top executives. It was during these times he would be visited by the devil on his shoulder telling him, "If these important people ever find out who you really are, you're toast." He told me he often still felt like an 18-year-old kid wearing cutoffs and flip-flops.

Sound familiar? Everyone I've ever told this to ends up smiling and nodding his or her head. We're really not that different from one another. Every one of us has insecurities—secrets we're afraid others will discover, and then—well, then, they'll know the real us.

Another one of those undeniable truths of life that has played out in my experience is, "People are not as smart as you think they are." Most of us are really good at putting others up on a pedestal because they seem to be so talented, smart, experienced or whatever. But when you eventually get to know them you realize, they're human, just like the rest of us.

My career took me from college to a small horse breeder's journal (I kid you not), that retail drug store chain and eventually to the big corporation, and I had a thought before making each move: I can't wait to work with a real company where people are smart and know what they're doing. And, without exception, I was shocked to find out that, regardless of the size of the company, people are just people. Some are smart, some, not so much. The older I get, the more people I meet, the more the adage proves itself. We're all just people trying to figure life out, one day at a time.

Life is made up of mistakes and surprises. For all of us. If we will beBRAVE! and show people the real us we may be surprised at the relief we see on their faces.

SPACE, THE FINAL FRONTIER

I'm going to close out this chapter on beBRAVE! with one of the most important concepts I've ever learned. I was first exposed to it in Stephen Covey's book *The 7 Habits of Highly Effective People*. It is summed up in this phrase: "Between stimulus and response, man has the freedom to choose."[6]

This idea was not original with Covey. It was first written about by Viktor Frankl, a psychiatrist imprisoned in the death camps of Nazi Germany. He suffered the loss of nearly his entire family and endured unimaginable torture and indignities. In the midst of this awful existence, Frankl discovered an important truth. Though his captors had control over his environment and what they could do to his body, there was a part of him they could not touch: his basic identity. Covey describes it this way, "He could decide within himself how all of this was going to affect him. Between what happened to him, or the stimulus, and his response to it, was his freedom or power to choose that response."

Think of it like this: if you pull hard on a dog's tail, it will turn around and bite you. The dog doesn't have the capacity to stop and think about what the appropriate response should be. Instinct drives behavior, and it turns to defend itself. It has no other choice. However, we as people are not like the dog. We are born with the ability to delay the response to what happens to us and to think about the best way to respond. Mind you, I'm not suggesting that we always use that ability, but it's there nonetheless. What Frankl discovered was that if he exercised that ability, over time it would grow. In the way a muscle breaks down when pushed hard, it would grow back bigger and stronger. The space expanded, which gave him more and more freedom to determine his response to whatever happened to him.

Life is stimulus. We are bombarded by it every waking moment. Most of the time, we are not in control of what we must confront everyday. Fear is a response. It wells up inside when we are faced with situations where it seems we have no control. Our freedom to choose our response lives in between the two. In that space is where we must turn the emotion of fear into information. In that space is where we are able to drain off our natural, emotional response to fear and replace it with a rational assessment of choices. Taming that wild frontier within us is one of the highest callings we have as human beings. Outer space is not the final frontier as Star Trek would have us believe; it is the inner space that exists between the things that happen to us and the way we choose to respond to them. How we develop that space will determine the course our lives will take. What we do with that space will determine whether we ever get to make that unique, creative contribution to the world.

BE CURIOUS BECAUSE DISCOVERY IS THE PATHWAY TO CREATIVITY.

8. BE CURIOUS!

"We keep moving forward, opening new doors,
and doing new things, because we're curious and
curiosity keeps leading us down new paths."
Walt Disney

WHAT IF...?

Hidden beneath one of the most visited tourist attractions in all the world, there exists a vibrant, hustling, bustling world that few have ever seen. It's comprised of rows upon rows of shiny offices, several cafeterias, a laundromat that washes upward of 285,000 pounds of clothes every day, a resident hairdresser, and much more. It took eight million cubic feet of earth and countless yards of concrete to build, and it continues to expand to this day. It's called the Utilidors (utility corridors) and can be found underneath Walt Disney World in Orlando, Florida.

The Utilidors are a great example of what happens when one person asks the question, "What if…?"

Walt Disney's first theme park, Disneyland in California, was a marvel of modern creativity and ingenuity. Scores of visitors passed through its gates every day, and by all accounts, it was a raving success. But, Walt Disney wasn't satisfied. He envisioned a magical place that would transport visitors from their own world to a world where anything could happen. As he evaluated his dream in operation, he was bothered by watching a cowboy striding through the futuristic Tomorrowland on his way to the bygone era of Frontierland. He felt that it ruined the experience. So, he asked, "What if I could find away for actors to move about the park without being seen?"

Disney soon realized that Disneyland was too small to do anything about it. So, he set his sights on a grander vision, a vision that would eventually become Walt Disney World (a world that, today, is larger than the city of San Francisco), a magical place where you will never see a cowboy traipsing through a sci-fi landscape.

There are few people in history who can overshadow the creative output of Walt Disney. Think about how different the world would be if he had never followed his inner curiosity. Curiosity continually propelled him to keep asking questions. It led him down unexpected roads of discovery. It was central to everything he eventually accomplished.

The beHABIT! of Adventure

beCURIOUS! is the beHABIT! of adventure. Embracing be-LIEVE! and beBRAVE! gives us the freedom to explore the world and rediscover the joy of learning. Have you ever witnessed the exhilaration on the face of an infant as he begins to learn about the world around him? This is what water feels like! This is how flowers smell! This is what birthday cake tastes like! It's that kind of excitement and enthusiasm that we want to rekindle with beCURIOUS!

Curiosity is the impulse to know things, to think new thoughts, to search out answers to questions we've been asking ourselves for years. Curiosity is the pathway to creativity. It is the road less taken. It shakes up our routine and gives us a fresh perspective on work and life.

Curiosity Is Hard

Some people are born with a natural bent toward adventure. When the opportunity to do something new presents itself, they are quick to pack a bag and be off. I've often admired these people, because I'm not one of them. Many creatives aren't. Often, part of the creative temperament is insecurity and the desire to seek out the quiet, comfortable places, where we can think and create at our own pace.

This is a problem. In our desire to stay with the familiar and build solid routine, we can learn to ignore spontaneity and avoid risk. It can even prevent us from learning from mistakes. In his own mind, Disney had failed with his initial vision. But, he used that failure to propel him to a new, much riskier, and grander effort. I mean, underground tunnels? Really?

Comfortable Misery

Burnout is not only the result of working too hard or neglecting our health. It also stems from doing the same work over and over again: working on the same accounts, writing the same articles, taking the same photographs, even driving the same way to work every day, day in and day out.

> *"The comfort of familiarity can be so alluring; even if it is not the best. I see countless people droning through their mundane lives, hanging on to their comfortable misery and blocking the thrill of new and unrealized but available successes."*
> Dan Miller

Routine is an important part of a balanced, creative life. But, when it becomes "comfortable misery," routine can be a creativity-killer.

I've recently noticed a trend in my own behavior. Now in my mid-50s, I find that I am always looking for ways to streamline my daily routine; setting out clothes the night before, organizing my toiletries in order of use, buying the same brand of T-shirts in varying colors. When I noticed that my hair was starting to thin, I shaved my head so I could get ready faster in the mornings. (Consult someone you trust before laying razor to scalp! Not all heads are created equal.) Some of you are thinking, Hey, that's nothing weird. I've been laying out my clothes the night before for years! I bring this up for one reason. If we're not careful, our attempt at building helpful, streamlining routines can take us to a place we don't really want to go, a place of comfortable misery.

Daily Curiosity

As with all the beHABITS!, change is often incremental. If you've ever wondered what it's like to skydive, it doesn't mean you have to jump out of an airplane this afternoon. There are endless ways of gently infusing your day with curiosity.

- If your creative process is most often worked alone, try inviting someone else to join you
- Find a different route to work (even if it takes longer)
- Pick a subject you've always wanted to know more about and Google it! (e.g. "tunnels under Disney World!")
- Try one restaurant a month that you've never been to before
- Ask yourself one "What if…?" question every morning as you start your day
- Make that call about skydiving lessons (just saying)

beCURIOUS!

beCURIOUS! extends a challenge for us to fight mundane routine. We do not need to be satisfied with the status quo. If we will just begin to ask a few more questions and then ferret out the answers, who knows what new paths we might find ourselves exploring?

be PLAYFUL!

BE PLAYFUL AND SEE THE WORLD THROUGH
THE EYES OF A CHILD. AGAIN.

9. bePLAYFUL!

"It is a happy talent to know how to play."
Ralph Waldo Emerson

EVERYDAY DELIGHT

Recently, I watched a short video that one of my Facebook friends posted. It's called "Rubber Band Babies."[1] It shows two diaper-clad toddlers delighting themselves with trying to put a rubber band around the knob of a kitchen cabinet and then pulling on it to see it snap. The absolute glee in their giggles made me laugh until I cried! Each of them had a rubber band and his own knob, and they were just as engaged in each other's successful snapping as in their own.

That's what bePLAYFUL! is all about: finding delight in everyday things.

I've learned more about play from my children than from anywhere else. When they were young, my wife and I encouraged a lot of imaginative play. Staples in our home included the dress-up box filled with old prom dresses, ties, shoes, hats and all manner of goofy things; a big box of large cardboard bricks (remember those?); a Fisher-Price kitchen (complete with food); and lots of other stuff. I would often arrive home from work to find my four kiddos acting out one of many fanciful stories. There were princesses (I have three daughters), superheroes, and knights in shining armor (the son). If I happened to wander on stage at just the right moment, I became the fire-breathing monster trying to burn everyone to a crisp!

Even now that they're adults, my children still remind me of the benefits of playing games. My daughter Christy and her husband, Kyle, live about three hours away. When they come to visit, I can always count on them bringing along a new board game that they are currently crazy about. Whether it entails conquering the world, building a railroad, or defeating a global pandemic, we all end up around the kitchen table laughing, telling stories, and just having a good time, (and saving the world, of course).

Children don't need to be taught how to play. It happens naturally. Sticks become swords; buckets of dirty water become stone soup; appliance boxes become rocket ships. Everything is an adventure, and the possibilities are endless.

> *"Men do not quit playing because they grow old;*
> *they grow old because they quit playing."*
> Oliver Wendell Holmes Jr.

Did you know that there is actually a National Institute for Play? That's right. There are some really smart people in the world who believe that play isn't just about having fun. Play might actually be the key to a better society and world! Their vision statement reads, "We envision a...future in which the science of human play enables individuals, parents, teachers, leaders, and organizations to harness the power of play to create transformational differences in their individual, family, school, and organizational lives."[2]

I can't say whether playfulness is going to save the world, but I can tell you that it has played a major role in my recovery from burnout. Remember that sketchbook my wife brought me while I was in the "joint"? I began to draw cartoons about some of my activities. It was dark humor, to be sure, but it was a playful act. (One depicted the perky activity director asking a group of us if we wanted to play a game of "coping skills" hangman. I didn't show it to the perky activity director.) I was trying to find the humor in my captivity and surroundings. I am convinced that there is humor in the darkest of places and circumstances. It's often subtle, but it's there. Seeking it out can sometimes be the difference between life and death.

LAUGHTER IS NOT A CONTROLLED SUBSTANCE

We've all heard that "laughter is the best medicine," but did you know that aside from lifting our emotions a bit, there are actual physical benefits to laughing? The Mayo Clinic writes that laughter can not only soothe tension and relieve stress, but it can also relieve pain, improve immune response, and stimulate the heart, lungs and muscles while increasing the endorphins released by the brain.[3] Although there's no scientific proof that laughter and fun extend life, William Klemm, D.V.M., Ph.D., Professor of Neuroscience at Texas A&M University, points out in his article for Psychology Today[4] that many famous comedians from the past century lived longer-than-average lives:

- Bob Hope, 100
- George Burns, 100
- Phyllis Diller, 95
- Milton Berle, 94
- Victor Borge, 91
- Jimmy Durante, 87
- Groucho Marx, 87
- Jonathan Winters, 86

- Red Skelton, 84
- Rodney Dangerfield, 83
- Johnny Carson, 80
- Jack Benny, 80

Dr. Klemm observes, "One thing is for sure. Whether or not humor makes you live longer, it surely does make you live happier."

Without laughter and play our creative potential is stunted. Life is serious business, no question, but when that seriousness begins to define us, we lose touch with the child who lives in all of us, regardless of age. We need wonder. We need surprise. We need to laugh until our sides hurt. bePLAYFUL! encourages us to return to that innocence, to suspend our "adult pragmatism" and look at the world through a child's eyes. Again.

I've got a couple rubber bands. Let's head to the kitchen!

bePLAYFUL!

BE PRESENT BECAUSE MULTITASKEROS IS A MYTHICAL BEAST.

10. BE PRESENT!

"The point of power is always in the present moment."
Louise L. Hay

THERE BE MONSTERS HERE

Dan, a dear friend of mine, recently took his family on a trip to Ireland and Scotland. After their return, Anne and I had them over for dinner, and they showed us pictures from the trip. One of their excursions took them to the Scottish Highlands and the famous Loch Ness. Dan confessed to me that, even as a skeptic, he couldn't help stealing a glance out over the water just in case he might catch a glimpse of old Nessie.

We all love a good story, especially when it involves monsters. Cable TV is filled with programs dedicated to looking for conclusive evidence that will finally prove their existence. Bigfoot, The Kraken, and Nessie herself—we love the possibility that maybe, just maybe, they're real.

Well, I want to tell you about a mythical creature I've actually seen with my own eyes.

THE SIGHTING

It wasn't on a mist-covered mountain or the high seas that I first saw it. It was in a meeting.

Meetings play a big role in my day job as an executive creative director—project meetings, brainstorming meetings, client meetings. This was the setting where I made that first sighting.

The meeting began with someone sharing the agenda. Data was passed out, explanations given, feedback requested. And, there it was, seated right at the table with us. Its bloodshot eyes were glued to its laptop, the clickety-clacking of claws on the keyboard filled the room. It was Multitaskeros, the mythical beast that believes it can do more than one thing at a time with precision and excellence. Its gaze occasionally scanned the table. There was a nod of the head—a mumbled "uh-huh" and "that's right" then back to the screen and claws flying.

Have you ever seen one? Have you ever *been* one? Of course you have. We all have. We become a Multitaskeros when we try to half-listen to what people are saying while thinking about where we're going for lunch while peeking at email or taking a call.

> *"Multitasking gives us all the opportunity*
> *to screw up more than one thing at a time."*
> Steve Uzell

In a recent survey, 92% of participants admitted to multitasking during meetings and 41% confessed to doing it "often" or "all the time."[1] For those of us who waste a lot of time in meetings, that comes as no surprise. Some companies have implemented a "no screen" policy for meetings in an attempt to stem the tide of constant distraction. What we can't seem to understand is that multitasking is a myth.

REAL MULTITASKING

The first use of the word "multitask" appeared in an IBM document back in 1965.[2] It referred to a microprocessor's ability to process several tasks at once. But here's the irony—in single processor computers, there is no real multitasking. Only one task can be processed at a time. The advantage computers provide is that they can switch between tasks many times per second, giving the appearance of multitasking. So, even at the time the word was coined, multitasking was a myth.

> *"[Multitasking is a] mythical activity in which people believe*
> *they can perform two or more tasks simultaneously."*
> Dr. Edward Hallowell

Today, the term has morphed into a "skill" that I often see on resumes. But, science has shown again and again that our brains just don't work that way.

THE TROUBLE WITH MULTITASKING

According to Psychologist David Meyer of the University of Michigan, the brain cannot fully focus when multitasking. In fact, people take longer to complete tasks. It can take up to twice as long compared to doing one thing at a time.[3] René Marois, a psychologist at Vanderbilt University, discovered that our brains exhibit a "response selection bottleneck" when trying to perform multiple tasks at once. When that happens, our brains have to decide which task should take priority, and that takes more time.[4] In fact, researchers from the University of California at Irvine[5] reported that, when distracted from a single task, it can take, on average, 25 minutes to return focus to the original task!

We are wired to focus on one thing at a time. When we distract ourselves with more than that, our concentration is fragmented, and none of what we're trying to accomplish gets the attention it deserves. And, here's a big surprise: Dr. Meyer suggests that, when we multitask, we are more likely to make mistakes—a lot more mistakes.

Wasted time and more mistakes aren't the worst part of multitasking.

Stress: The Real Monster

If Multitaskeros is a mythical beast, than what's the real monster? Stress.

In today's rapid-fire world, many of us have fallen for the lie that in order to be productive, or even prolific, we must master the "art" of doing more than one thing at a time. For some people, the penalty is just wasted time and reduced productivity. For creatives, however, the penalty can be much worse. In his bestselling book *The Accidental Creative*, Todd Henry says, "You need to create space for your creative process to thrive rather than expect it to operate in the cracks of your frenetic schedule."[6] Frenetic is the perfect word to use when it comes to multitasking. The word derives from Middle English (frenetik) and literally means insane!

When the demands on our time and attention exceed our ability to respond effectively, our brains do the best they can to help. They pump adrenaline and other stress hormones into our systems. These hormones provide a quick burst of energy, but in the end, more energy does not help us multitask. It just produces stress. And, for the creative professional, stress can quite literally be a killer, or as Todd Henry says, "An assassin to creativity."

The Creative Cost

bePRESENT! is the habit of doing one thing at a time—the habit of focused attention. In the hit TV show M*A*S*H,[7] there was a character named Charles Emerson Winchester III, a blue blooded, arrogant smarty-pants from Boston—a brilliant surgeon dumped into a Mobile Army Surgical Hospital (MASH) unit in the middle of the Korean War. There, speed was the key, not technical skill. But, in his first episode, Dr. Winchester proclaimed, "I do one thing at a time. I do it very well. And I move on." Charles was on to something there.

The energy that those hormones dump into our systems doesn't go to helping us accomplish more than one thing at a time. Instead, it fuels stress and anxiety, which rob our ability to focus. The added stress and anxiety often syphon off energy stores that we need to create. Our precious ability to be creative is all about seeing the world differently. We see what everyone else sees but are able to see beyond the surface and think more deeply about it. We're able to connect dots that most people don't even know are there. That process requires space to thrive. It won't happen in the "cracks" between checking Facebook, answering an email, and listening to phone messages. When we try to force creating into fragmented, incongruent slivers of time, the screen stays blank, and the page stays empty, as our thoughts bounce around like balls in a pinball machine.

What Does bePRESENT! Look Like?

The concept behind bePRESENT! is simple: we focus on what's in front of us to the exclusion of other distractions. Oh, if only it were that easy! Focused attention is like a muscle. It has to be exercised over and over again in order to become strong and reliable. In our frenzied culture, that is not an easy habit to form. However, the benefits that come from making the effort to bePRESENT! are worth it.

Emotional Oxygen

When talking to someone face-to-face, look her in the eyes. Put away the phone, close the laptop, and focus on what she's saying to you. In his book The 7 Habits of Highly Effective People, Stephen Covey's Habit 5 is: "Seek first to understand, then to be understood."[8] When someone is talking to me, I many times begin to formulate a response while he is talking! I'm not really listening. I'm more concerned about responding than listening. But, we can all tell when we're not being heard. The person we're trying to communicate with is fidgeting with his phone. His eyes flit over our shoulder at something or someone behind us. We don't get any acknowledgment of what we're actually saying—maybe a grunt or quick nod. That's not being understood.

> *"Listening for deep understanding is the key to influence with others and to true creativity and innovation.*
> *When you really listen to another person from their point of view, and reflect back to them that understanding, it's like giving them emotional oxygen."*
> Stephen Covey

I love that term, "emotional oxygen." There is no greater satisfaction than knowing you've been heard and understood. It ushers in a peace that allows for greater understanding and communication. A truly human connection occurs, forming a wonderful foundation upon which to share your thoughts and build collaboration.

A Quiet Space

Our lives are filled with noise, and much of it is self-generated. We turn on the TV in the morning. We stick our earphones in when taking a walk. We listen to the news or music on the drive to work. It's as if we were afraid of the quiet. Maybe we are. In the stillness, when we're left with our own thoughts, things that have been pushed aside tend to surface, scary things, hurtful things, stressful things. For a time these things can be pushed beneath a constant stream of sound, but, they're not really gone. Those thoughts and fears are there, generating stress and distraction every minute of every day, stifling our creative potential and frustrating our ability to contribute at a high level.

When I make the effort to turn off the outer distractions, I often find a different type of noise bubbling to the surface: my own jumbled thoughts. Quiet invites those random, disconnected worries and to-dos to step to the front of my mind and overwhelm me. This is a common situation, especially with creatives. In her bestselling book *The Artist's Way*, Julia Cameron describes a morning ritual she calls Morning Pages.

"Morning Pages provoke, clarify, comfort, cajole, prioritize, and synchronize the day at hand. Do not over-think Morning Pages: just put three pages of anything on the page…and then do three more pages tomorrow."[9]

Morning Pages is a continuous stream-of-consciousness style of writing. There's no editing, no stopping, it's all in longhand, for three pages. Write down the tasks, fears, honey-dos, bills to be paid, commitments you've made…anything and everything that comes to mind. Be patient in starting this exercise. Nothing may come to mind at first. But, if you wait in the stillness, things will begin trickling out of your mind. They will begin to flow more and more easily. Before you know it, you'll have filled your three pages with things that were swimming inside your head. Now that they're out, it's much easier (and less scary) to move into the day and bePRESENT!

SLAY THE MULTITASKEROS!

bePRESENT! is a call to action for those who create. It's a reminder to resist the temptation to become a Multitaskeros, and instead, to press calm and order into our life. This will require making a conscious decision, moment-by-moment, throughout the day. But it becomes easier over time. And the more we give each person and task the focused attention they deserve, the less likely it will be to have our inner Multitaskeros raise it's ugly head.

bePRESENT!

BE CONNECTED BECAUSE NO ARTIST, OR IDEA, IS AN ISLAND.

11. beCONNECTED!

*"I think it is in collaboration that
the nature of art is revealed."*
Steve Lacy

Hello Dear!

Once a week, I like to go to this little Chinese buffet just a few miles north of where I work. I go there for a few reasons. The food is good. The price is reasonable. It's close to the office. But none of those is the main reason I like to go to Two Brothers. Whenever I walk in the door, the proprietor greets me with a big smile and says, "Hello, dear!" She's a kindhearted, 30-something woman who speaks broken English and takes good care of all the lunchtimers who pass through her doors. Because of my weekly appearances (spread over several years), this nice lady knows me by sight and remembers that I always get takeout and a diet soda. When I walk in, she doesn't ask if I want a table. She doesn't ask if I want a drink. She just hands me the white Styrofoam container, smiles, and says "Hello, dear!" When I arrive at the register with my full container, sitting on the counter is my diet soda. We've never talked about anything more complicated than the weather, but there's always a smile, a little wave, and an "Enjoy you lunch, dear!" as I leave. There is a connection between us that is satisfying, at least to me. There's something special about just being recognized and remembered—a uniquely human connection.

The Human Connection

beCONNECTED! is the habit of human connection. Human

beings were meant for community. You've heard it takes a village to raise a child? Well, I'm here to tell you, it takes a village to keep you sane, especially those of us who create for a living. Our ideas are better when we can bounce them off each other. Our ability to solve problems is bolstered by sharing our thoughts with others—getting someone else's unique perspective. The creative process is about differing points of view colliding together to make unimagined possibilities.

However, the simple act of connecting with others doesn't come easily to some of us.

BEING AN INTROVERT

Are you an introvert or an extravert? This topic has gotten a lot of attention in recent years. It may stem from a delightful article entitled *Caring for Your Introvert* by Jonathan Rauch.[1] He defines the differences this way: "Extroverts are energized by people, and wilt or fade when alone…in contrast, after an hour or two of being socially 'on,' we introverts need to turn off and recharge." The first time I read that article, I thought, "Finally! Someone has put my own experience into words!" I am an introvert. I am comfortable speaking in front of large crowds, but I hate being at big parties. I enjoy a quiet conversation with a friend about important things, but I don't like small talk with strangers. If I am in a public situation for any length of time, I need quiet, alone time to recharge my batteries. It's not a personality disorder…it's the way I'm wired.

It's the way a lot of creative people are wired.

PEOPLE ARE HARD

There's something we (both extraverts and introverts alike) need to keep in mind as we put effort into connecting with others. People are hard. By that, I mean that relationships are never easy. They are fragile, complicated, and often unpredictable. Being connected with others takes intentional, determined commitment and a long view of the benefits to us and to those with whom we connect. I have a Peanuts cartoon on my wall at work where the blanket-toting character, Linus, sums up people and relationships quite succinctly. "I love mankind, it's the people I can't stand." Unfortunately, it's the people that we must connect with. One thing that makes it hard is the false expectation that it isn't hard, but easy.

In 1971 Coca-Cola ran a television commercial entitled, *I'd Like to Teach the World to Sing (In Perfect Harmony)*.[2] It pictured a multicultural group of teenagers on top of a hill, standing side-by-side, each holding a bottle of Coke. It is now considered to be one of the most iconic spots in advertising history. The song became so popular that it was rerecorded by a group called The New Seekers from the UK and released on a vinyl 45. The simple message was that all we need to do is buy the world a Coke, teach them a simple song, and we will have peace and harmony on earth. Sounds simple enough.

If only…

Marketing does that. It makes complex challenges appear to be simple to solve. If you're overweight, take a pill. If you're in debt, make a phone call. If you're looking for your lifelong love, go to this website.

> *"For every complex problem there is an answer*
> *that is clear, simple, and wrong."*
> H. L. Mencken

Don't get me wrong, I have nothing against online dating sites or people that use them. In fact, I have several family members that have met their lifelong loves through these websites. But the key word in that last sentence is "met." Websites like Match.com and e-Harmony do a great job at helping you meet someone you have a lot in common with. But whether or not that introduction blossoms into a serious, lasting relationship is totally up to the people involved.

Utopian Aspirations

The quaint little town of New Harmony, Indiana is about 40 miles northwest from where I live. It is a cultural gem and popular destination for many site seers, picnickers and wedding goers each year. According to the 2010 census, New Harmony has around 800 fulltime residents. The town has a fascinating history out of which came: the first free library, one of the first civic drama clubs and a public school system open to both men and woman.

A man by the name of Robert Owen founded New Harmony in 1825. He purchased the land from the Harmony Society who had originally settled there. His vision was to create a utopian society of "happiness, enlightenment, and prosperity through education, science, technology, and communal living."[3] Owen invited "any and all" to come join him in this sincere undertaking. Within a few months, New Harmony had fallen into chaos and economic failure. In 1826 splinter groups dissatisfied with the how things were developing, broke away eventually leading to smaller communities and further subdivision.

Apparently, utopia is hard.

Throughout human history, people have tried to build the perfect society. The fact that none of them have flourished for any length of time is telling. The problem with building utopia is that the building blocks have to be people. And, well, people are hard. Perhaps, if Owen had had a few bottles of Coke on hand and a catchy song to teach everyone, he might have had a better outcome. Or not.

Despite that fact that relationships are hard, we are still left with the undeniable truth that connection with others is indispensable to a life of healthy, prolific, creative contribution. I know this to be true first hand, because I tried it the other way.

Creating in a Vacuum

In the fall of 1996 I left the day-to-day, workaday world to try working at home. I claimed one of the four bedrooms in our house and set up my studio: a few build-it-yourself desks and cabinets, a new office chair, a couple computers, a phone, and an ISDN connection to the Internet (do they even have those anymore?). I could hardly wait to start my first day! I stayed in my sweats and slippers (just because I could), turned up my music, and reveled in not having to interact with anyone. It was quite the head rush for an introvert.

For a time, it was a pretty sweet deal. I was able to concentrate better and get more done in less time. There were no distractions, no one dropping in to say hi or chat about the weekend. I could stay focused on the work, talk on the phone when necessary, and do most of my communicating through email. The time flew by as my workdays grew longer and my night times grew shorter. I was in the groove. This went on for over four years.

I'll never do that again.

After the newness of the situation wore off, things began to change. My productivity declined. My creative muscles seemed fatigued, as generating new ideas became more of a chore than a delight. The workload was a never-ending burden that would keep me in my chair from early morning until late in the evening. I was working 18-hour days and most weekends. The very thing I thought would bring me ultimate freedom was beginning to feel more like a prison—like solitary confinement. I had become more and more reclusive (which is hard to do with a wife and four active children). It led to depression, declining physical health, and apathy about life.

After those four years, the agency I had worked for prior to heading out on my own asked if I'd like to come back. I jumped at the chance. I was done with being alone every day. I was hungry for people. I was starving for conversation and the sharing of ideas.

And then I remembered…people are hard.

It was a rough transition. I had to force myself to get used to the interruptions: someone stopping by to ask if I'd seen Monday Night Football, people talking and laughing a little too loudly in the cubical next door, meetings that could have been avoided with a group email. (And…I had to wear pants!) The first month was tough. But then I began to notice some changes. I was feeling better, lighter. I became more involved, engaged, and energized. My work began to improve, and the act of creating became fun again. Was it easy to reengage? No. Was it worth the effort? Without question!

You Can't Breathe in a Vacuum

beCONNECTED! reminds us that no artist, or idea, is an island. We are better artists—better people—when we engage with each other. I still enjoy the quiet and find refreshment when I'm alone. But now I know that my connection to the world around me is literally creative oxygen. Ideas are often hatched in quiet, alone time, but they grow and develop when shared with others.

"Creativity is just connecting things."
Steve Jobs

Burnout takes on many different looks in many different situations. In my experience, it is never more apt to harass our creative souls than when we isolate ourselves from the world. When we allow ourselves to drift away from interacting with others, we lose sight of the value, the joy, the creative spark that comes from a genuine human connection. The world and our perceived reality can get distorted. People need people. Creatives need other creatives. It's the only way we can maintain balanced, healthy lives.

Today at lunch, let's meet a couple miles north of Diamond Avenue and grab takeout from Two Brothers. You never know just how much a "Hello, dear!" can change your entire outlook on life.

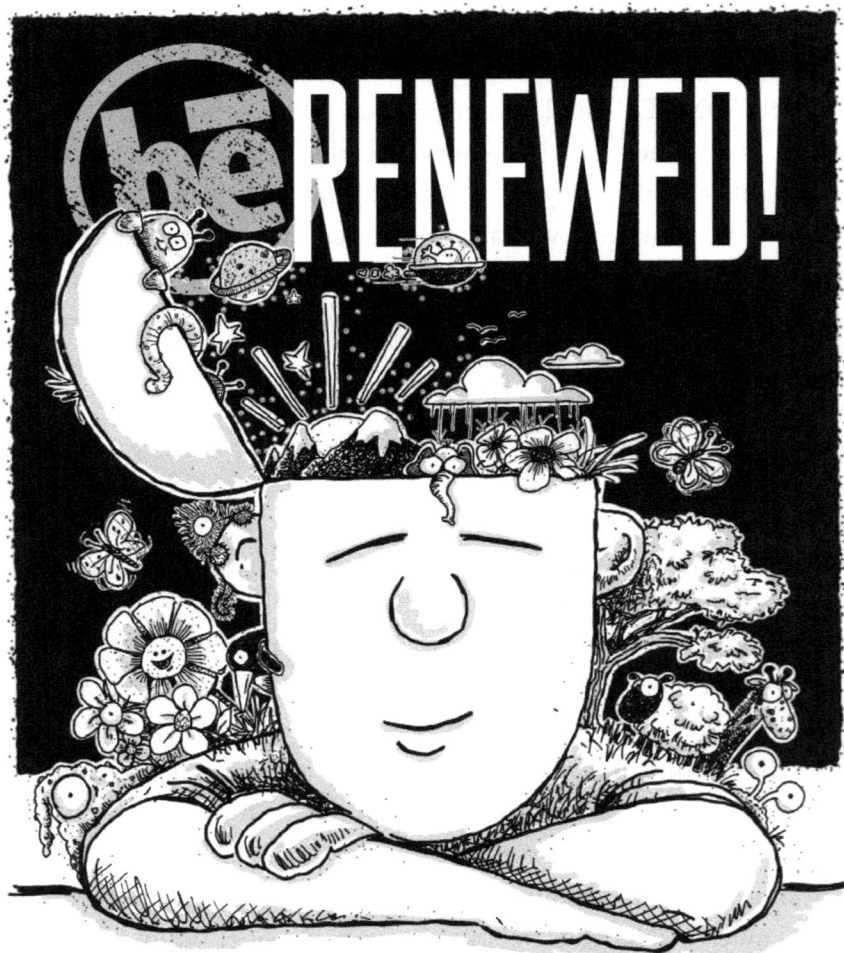

beRENEWED!

BE RENEWED BECAUSE CREATIVITY REQUIRES PHYSICAL, EMOTIONAL AND SPIRITUAL HEALTH TO THRIVE.

12. BE RENEWED

*"As I leave the garden I take with me
a renewed view, and a quiet soul."*
Jessica Coupe

LESSONS FROM AN AXE

Abraham Lincoln is often credited with saying, "Give me six hours to chop down a tree, and I will spend the first four sharpening the axe." He knew that having a sharp blade makes all the difference when it comes to downing a tree. (So does the name and number of a good tree service!) The concept here is pretty straightforward. To be well-equipped for the work at hand, we must invest time in preparation. And, just as important, we must know when to stop swinging the axe so it can be sharpened again.

How often do we force ourselves to keep working on a solution long after our "creative axe" is dull from overuse? Somewhere in our brains there's a little voice telling us just to try harder, push a little longer. One more cup of coffee, and the answer will come. Sometimes an acceptable answer does come, but at what cost?

THE LAW OF THE FARM

beRENEWED! is the restating of a familiar concept sometimes referred to as the law of the farm. If you want to reap a harvest, you first have to prepare the ground, plant the seeds, and nurture the crop over time. Skip any one of those steps, and there's no harvest. No amount of concerted effort, positive thinking, or stomping up and down will change that fact. Certain things just have to happen if we want other things to be possible. This is a natural principle.

It's like gravity. Gravity exists and exerts its influence on us, whether or not we believe or acknowledge it.

African Violet

My mother loved plants. She always had a variety of different flowers in our home. One of her favorites was the African violet. African violets are a hardy flower, and if you take care to water them and expose them to sunlight, they'll last forever. And, just one leaf can give birth to an entirely new plant! That's pretty amazing when you think about it. She once gave me a leaf of my own in its own pot. It came with simple instructions to keep it alive and thriving. I followed those instructions and I had a very nice-looking African violet that I took to work and put on the window ledge facing north.

Then, I forgot about the simple instructions. For a time, my African violet did fine. Then, it had fewer and fewer blossoms. Eventually, it stopped blooming all together. Then it was a pretty decent green plant for a while. It never complained. It never threw anything at me to remind me to take care of it. It just slowly withered and eventually died. One day, a co-worker of mine noticed the pathetic plant, marched into my office and, without a single word, took it away.

A few weeks later, I happened to stop in to that co-worker's office and noticed a beautiful, blooming plant on her windowsill. I made a comment about how lovely it was and she said, "That's the one you almost killed." I was shocked! It was much bigger, covered with blooms, and most certainly not dead! She told me that if I promised to be more careful, she would give me a leaf to start over.

A Renewable Resource

By the grace of God, creativity is a renewable resource. It's not a finite substance like oil or time, which, once burned, is gone. Creativity is more like an African violet. If consistently cared for and nurtured, it will thrive. It will bloom again and again.

But, it must be nurtured.

Funny thing, nurturing: it doesn't happen on it's own. It doesn't take care of itself. Unless we make a concerted effort to plan and then carry out the act of nurturing something, it will eventually die.

> *"You need to cultivate your own Central Park."*
> Jon Acuff, *Start*

In his best selling book, *Start*, Jon Acuff tells the story of when he had recently returned from a wonderful vacation on the beach with his wife and kids. He had disconnected from his normal craziness and spent time building sand castles and having meaningful, un-rushed conversations. He'd returned full of life. Jon relayed his excitement to his friend, Al Andrews who, of course, was very happy for him. But then Al said, "That's great! How do you do that next month without a beach? How do you make sure you don't kill yourself for fifty weeks of the year with the hope that you can make it to those two weeks of vacation?"[1]

Answer: cultivate your own Central Park.

Jon's friend used New York City as a metaphor for life. Central Park is a vast expanse of green in the middle of miles and miles of concrete and buildings. Too often we pour concrete and build buildings over every part of our lives leaving no room for a Central Park, no sanctuary in our days, weeks, or months. A two-week vacation once a year is nice, but it won't sustain us over the long haul. beRENEWED! Reminds us that renewal has to come in more frequent, less grand ways to be genuinely effective.

What Does Your Park Look Like?

Just as burnout expresses itself differently in each of us, so too does our Central Park. Does yours have a pond or a lake? Maybe it has a winding path or a mountain trail? Perhaps your park isn't even outside, but looks like a cozy couch by a fire or a good book and a back porch swing. The activities and surroundings of beRE-NEWED! are as varied and unique as we are, but the need to have a place to find refreshment and renewal is the same for all of us.

In conversations I've had with hundreds of creatives, there have been a few common themes when it comes to renewal. I'll list a few here, just to give you a place to start.

Journal

There's something about the feel of a leather-bound journal in your hands. It just seems to invite you to settle in and re-flect—to share your inner-most thoughts and feelings. Writing your thoughts out longhand is a great way to uncover things that might be caus-ing anxiety and stress. Getting the words out of our heads and onto the page in front of us can be very therapeutic. It can also make big issues take their proper size and proportion to the rest of our life. I recommend

you find a journal that will lay flat (like a Moleskin) and a nice pen (currently I'm using the Sharpie Pen, fine tip). Make the process of writing out your thoughts, feelings, and dreams a luxurious and inviting activity.

WALK

Physical activity is an essential ingredient in beRENEWED!. The act of putting our screens, keyboards, and phones away and taking to the streets is a great way to unwind and give our brains a break. There are obvious physical and health benefits, but it will also help to sharpen our thinking and decision-making. Recent studies are showing that even short walks done on a regular basis are helpful. So don't be put off by the idea that it has to be a marathon to be beneficial.

FIELD TRIP

Remember how fun the occasional field trip was in grade school? Instead of sitting at our desks working on spelling tests and math problems, we climbed on to the bus and headed off to some new and exciting place. I remember one trip from my own childhood in upstate New York—the Seward House. William Seward served as Secretary of State in the Lincoln and Johnson administrations. He's also the guy who arranged for the U.S. to acquire Alaska. His house, converted into a museum, was filled with all kinds of interesting memorabilia and historically significant artifacts. I still recall it fondly some 40 years later!

Field trips are not just for grade-school kids. Google a few points of interest around you. Pick one that sounds interesting and plan an outing, either alone or with a friend, and go exploring! The change of scenery and learning new things can be very inspiring.

Unplug

Technology has taken over our lives. Think about how many hours a day we spend staring at one kind of a screen or another. It's really mind-boggling! We have instant access to avalanches of information and creative tools that we couldn't have dreamed of just 10 years ago. But it can also become overwhelming—even mind-numbing. Look at your calendar, pick a weekend and declare it "My Unplugged Weekend." Force yourself (and I do mean force!) to leave the phone off, the TV off, the computer off. Instead of staring into the soft glow of our many digital companions, reconnect with the humans in our lives: spouse, kids, friends, even siblings (no, really). Engage in conversations instead of texting. Talk about life over coffee instead of catching up with Facebook. Pick up a pencil and paper to write or sketch instead of a stylus and your iPad (toughest one for me!). Unplugging from technology can really help to stimulate our creative juices.

Nap

There is nothing more satisfying than taking a nap on a lazy Sunday afternoon (when there's no football to watch, I mean). Whether it's your bed, a La-Z-Boy or even a soft blanket on the grass, the point is to rest. We Americans are sleep-deprived. The incidents of burnout and depression track inversely with the decline in quality sleep. Even a 20-minute power nap can make a big difference in our ability to think creatively and critically.

BEDTIME

Speaking of being sleep-deprived, the "Sleep in America" polls[2]—conducted on behalf of the National Sleep Foundation—tell us that about 20% of Americans report getting less than 6 hours of sleep a night, and the number of people reporting that they get 8 hours or more is on a rapid decline. The polls and several large studies have linked sleep deficits with poor work performance, driving accidents, relationship problems, and mood problems like anger and depression. Lack of sleep plays an enormous role in burnout. Conversely, that means that one sure way to beRENEWED! is to be more diligent about getting the rest we need. Remember that little voice inside telling us to "try harder and push a little longer"? Give it a good punch in the throat. Avoid caffeine too late in the day. Stop working or watching TV at least an hour before bed. Experiment with various routines that can help you ease into your night's sleep. Those extra hours of shuteye will feel wonderful the next day.

DIET

We are what we eat. I hate that phrase, but it's true. If we're not eating at least a semi-healthy diet, we're not going to function at our best. The human body is a machine—an engine. It runs on fuel like any other engine. The higher the quality of that fuel, the more efficiently and effectively the engine will run. Now, I know there are many opinions out there about what actually constitutes a "healthy" diet, and many of them contradict one another. It can be very frustrating to figure out how to eat for optimum health. The older I get, the more I believe that "moderation in all things" is the best advice for eating (and every other part of life, for that matter). More fruits and vegetables, less pizza and cake. And, let's not forget that the green M&Ms count as vegetables. No, really.

ROUTINE

Human beings are creatures of habit. Most of us function better with healthy routines pressed into our daily lives. A morning routine for getting up, waking up and getting ready for the day can actually clear away the cobwebs. A daily routine for organizing our thoughts and activities at work or home can make us more productive. An evening routine can help us unwind, pack away our concerns from the day and ease into a good night's sleep. Don't think of the word "routine" as rigid and confining. Healthy routines are a way of organizing our many responsibilities into manageable chunks. They don't have to be identical every day. Think of them as guardrails that keep you going in the same general direction, but allow flexibility to respond to the unexpected. The vast majority of creatives I know say that routine is an essential component of their ability to create and contribute at a high level.

THE COMMON THREAD

Do you notice a common thread running through these suggestions? None of them happen by accident. Renewal is like that. If we want to make our unique, creative contributions over the long haul, we have to be the kind of person who will beRENEWED! on purpose. For many of us, that requires constant effort to try new things and a willingness to change.

Our path to experiencing continual renewal begins with asking ourselves a simple, but hard question: am I willing to change?

beRENEWED!

be GRATEFUL!

Be grateful because it frees us to be wildly creative and live life with intentionality and joy.

13. BE GRATEFUL!

"Gratitude is not only the greatest of virtues,
but the parent of all the others."
Cicero

The Center of the Universe

Chances are, at one point in your life, you were a teenager. Teenagers are an interesting lot. I know because I've not only been one, I've helped raise four of them. Teenagers are real life Dr. Jekylls and Mr. Hydes. One minute they can be kind and friendly, the next, angry and reclusive. We all go through it: hormones flooding our developing brains, needing the help and support of our parents but wanting desperately to make our own way in the world. It's amazing that any of us survive to adulthood.

One thing that all teenagers share in common is the lens through which they see the world. They sit in the center of the universe, and everything else in all creation surrounds them with the sole purpose of serving their needs. It is all about them. With each of our four, Anne and I had to continually remind each other that it was just a phase…eventually they'd grow out of it and begin to realize their proper place in the cosmos. Until then, there they'd sit with unrealistically high expectations about what life owes them: a girlfriend, a boyfriend, a car, a later curfew, a better grade, a higher allowance, the new iPhone, blah, blah-blah, blah-blah.

But, have you noticed? There are some grown-ups who seem to have gotten stuck in their teenage years. They look all grown up on the outside, but inside they're still under the impression that their rightful spot in the world is front and center. We all know one or two. And, if we're really honest with ourselves, we still take a seat on that throne now and again.

The Law of Attraction

There is a popular philosophy in our culture today referred to as "the law of attraction." It's an idea that's been around since people first walked the planet and surfaces periodically in books and blogs. The concept is simple, think about wealth, and you will become wealthy. Picture a brand-new car in your head, and soon it will be parked in your driveway. You deserve a high-paying job, so just think about the dollar amount you want. Write it down. Stick it to the bathroom mirror. Keep that number in your conscious mind, and you will attract the perfect job right to you.

There's another phrase for the law of attraction: a life of entitlement.

The Trouble with Entitlement

A life of entitlement sounds pretty sweet on the surface, but in reality, it's a very hard way to live. It sets us up for a series of never-ending disappointments and frustrations. What happens when the things we want and deserve never show up? And, how do we respond when all those things that we don't want come marching through our front doors?

Here are just a few things that we might feel entitled to:

- Happiness
- Health
- Good relationships
- Great job

- Money (lots of it)
- Influence
- Success (however it's defined)
- Nice house
- Nice car
- All the toys we want (because so-and-so has it)
- All the food we can eat (in unlimited varieties)
- Clean fresh water (duh!)
- Big vacations
- Fashionable clothes (and new ones as the styles change, of course)
- Wisdom and insight that others want to hear

Every item on that list, by definition, presents an opportunity for disappointment and frustration.

- Why am I not happy?
- Why did this illness happen to me?
- Why does nobody like me?
- Why did I get stuck in this lousy job?
- I'm sick and tired of not having the money I deserve!
- No one listens to a word I say!
- Why does everyone else get the good jobs, and I get stuck just chasing my tail?
- Why do I have to live in this poor excuse for a house?
- My other car should be a Porsche!
- Geez! Why can't I have the new iPod? All my friends have it!
- What do you mean we have to eat meatloaf again?
- I want bottled water, not that swill that comes from the tap!

- What? I'm not going to Disney World? Everyone goes to Disney World!
- These jeans are so yesterday! I need the new ones that are all torn up at the knees!
- I'm not going to throw my pearls of wisdom before swine!
- IT'S...NOT...FAIR!

CREATIVITY-KILLER

The life of entitlement is a creativity-killer, plain and simple. Trying to figure out why life has been unfair at every turn takes up so much time and energy, there just isn't enough left to beCURIOUS! or bePLAYFUL! Entitlement is so all-consuming that it overshadows everything. Even the good things that happen aren't quite good enough. Life becomes a never-ending pursuit of things that are always just out of reach. The concept of contentment is thought of as failure—giving up on your dreams. And in the process, the needs of others go entirely unnoticed. In fact, entitlement so totally saturates a person's thoughts that the idea of actually contributing something to benefit others is completely off the radar. The reason for living is diminished to just wanting and getting, wanting and getting, wanting and getting.

A BEAUTIFUL EVENING

Recently, Anne shared a friend's Facebook post with me. It read, "It's a beautiful evening. The parking lot lights are shimmering, the band at the [restaurant] across the highway is playing some '60s music." It sounded like a couple out on the town, enjoying themselves at a popular hangout, maybe meeting up with friends for a drink or dinner—just a pleasant evening that someone wanted to share via a Facebook post and photo.

Here's the rest of the post: "…and we are here at the IGA fixing the car. Happy Friday night!"

> *"Either I see all of life as a gift, or I demand that life have a certain look to it."*
> Paul Miller, *A Praying Life*

Wait, what? At the IGA fixing the car? The photo that accompanied the post was of the woman's husband, hood on the car up, bent over the engine. Was he frustrated or upset that while "everyone else" was having a good time on a Friday night, he and his wife were stuck in a grocery store parking lot, fixing their car? Nope. He's smiling and giving a thumbs-up to his wife.

Gratitude and Contentment

beGRATEFUL! is the habit of living life with gratitude and contentment. It's not defeatism. It's not fatalism. It's not playing the role of a martyr. It's not pretending that life is never hard. Of course life is hard sometimes. Life is tragic and painful sometimes. Approaching life with a Pollyannaish optimism is no better than feeling entitled. Both perspectives are skewed pictures of reality, and neither is sustainable.

To the contrary, a life lived with a grateful heart is one of peace. It is a life of clarity and contribution. Every circumstance has a purpose, every opportunity a blessing. beGRATEFUL! changes the trajectory of life itself. If entitlement kills creativity, then gratitude feeds it. Gratitude provides the inner strength to beLIEVE!, beBRAVE!, beCURIOUS!, bePLAYFUL!, bePRESENT!, be-CONNECTED and beRENEWED! It is the mortar between the bricks of a creative life well-lived.

Space, the Final Frontier

Remember the concept from beBRAVE!? There is a space between the things that happen to us and the response we have to them. That space is the key to gratitude, just as it is to being brave. Here's the key phrase again: "Between stimulus and response, man has the freedom to choose."[1]

The freedom to choose. Between the things that happen to us and the way we respond is a space, and in that space is freedom to

choose our response, a freedom that is uniquely human. Just this week, I was having a conversation with a fellow creative about control, more precisely, how little control we have over life. But, what we do have control over mostly consists of how we respond to the things that happen (and don't happen). In that space is freedom.

I want to encourage you to look for that space today. When presented with the unexpected, take advantage of the space. Weigh the options before you. What response will strengthen your ability to create? What response will free you from the chains of resentment and bitterness? Use that space. Exercise your freedom. BeGRATEFUL!

YOUR WORLD IS WAITING.

14. Your World Is Waiting

"When you cease to make a contribution, you begin to die."
Eleanor Roosevelt

Will I Make The List?

If we were to compose a list of the most influential people who have ever lived, who would make the list? Let's say that we had to limit the list to twenty. Who would those 20 people be? And, what criteria would we use to judge their contributions? Well, as you would expect, when I Googled "Most influential people in history" it returned some 172,000,000 responses. I found a great list on Ranker.com.[1] The rankings are based on visitors to the site voting them up or down. Here is the criteria they cite: "This is a list of the most influential people of all of human history. This means that the individuals on this list have had a significant affect on how regular people live their lives today and have had a large impact on how modern society works. The names on this list include religious figures, scientists and inventors, and some of the most important leaders in world history." This list changes as more people vote, but on the day I looked at it, this is the order I found. Drumroll, please...

1) Jesus Christ
2) Mohammad
3) Isaac Newton
4) Albert Einstein
5) Aristotle
6) Leonardo da Vinci
7) Galileo Galilei
8) Plato

9) Charles Darwin
10) Moses
11) Alexander the Great
12) Mahatma Gandhi
13) Socrates
14) Gautama Buddha (Buddha had a first name?)
15) Abraham Lincoln
16) Nikola Tesla
17) George Washington
18) Julius Caesar
19) Confucius
20) William Shakespeare

Now, obviously, this list isn't definitive. If I had chosen another Google response to highlight, there would be different names in a different order. But, overall, it's not bad. It would be hard to argue that these people didn't deserve to be on a list of this kind, in whatever order you placed them. They've all "had a large impact on how modern society works."

Now, you might be thinking, Ah, I know where he's going with this. He's going to make the point that these were all real people who didn't set out to change the world. They all just lived life and contributed as they could, and BAM! they changed the world!

That is one way to look at this list, but that's not where I'm going. This is a list of extremely influential people, and whether or not they set out to change the world as we know it, they changed it nonetheless. It would be easy to look at this list of 20 people, out of the estimated 110 billion who have ever lived, and think, *"Great…and I'm supposed to change the world from my little corner of it? Not likely."*

And you'd be right.

Your World

It's very unlikely that you or I are going to change the world or the course of history. An argument could be made that some of the people on the list above didn't either. In fact, there are people alive right now who have never heard the names on that list. The people on that list had an impact, no question, but did they all change the entire world?

When we set our sights on goals that are too big, we set ourselves up for disappointment and discouragement. Have you ever found yourself feeling helpless when watching an hour or two of world news? The sheer magnitude of human suffering, corrupt governments, and natural disasters can be overwhelming. If I'm not careful, I can slide into thinking that there is nothing I can do to help. What difference can it possibly make if I send $20 to the Red Cross or volunteer at the Christian Life Center down the street? It's like a single drop of rain in the middle of an endless desert.

Let me share one last concept from Stephen Covey and his *7 Habits of Highly Effective People.*[2] In chapter 1, Be Proactive, he describes two circles.

The inner circle, the Circle of Influence, is where things we can control reside—things like our attitudes, our choices and our

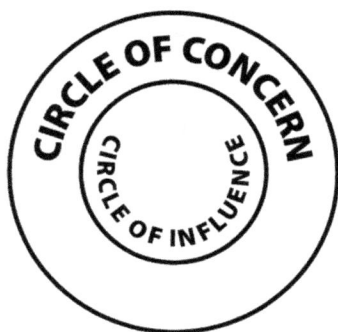

pursuits. In the outer circle, the Circle of Concern, live things that may trouble us but over which we have no influence or control: the weather, the national debt, unrest in the Middle East. If we spend time focused on the Circle of Concern, we can waste our lives fretting over things that are outside our reach. But if, instead, we spend our time on things in the smaller Circle of Influence, life takes on new possibilities. Inside that smaller circle, the $20 I send to the Red Cross and the hours volunteering at the Christian Life Center both matter and make a difference.

Now, the diagram of the 2 circles can be a little misleading—it's a bird's eye view. Looking down on the circles from that perspective can give the impression that those things in our Circle of Concern

are almost within our reach. I mean…it's just a thin line between my area of influence and all those other things that I could spend time thinking and worrying about. But if we could look at those "circles" from a different vantage point, they might look more like the picture on the previous page.

That "Circle" of Concern (and everything inside it) isn't within reach. In reality, those things are miles beyond our reach. Our world lives in the *smaller* circle. That's where we need to focus. That's where our unique, creative contributions will have impact. And, your world is different than my world. The things and people I have influence over are different from the things and people over which you have influence. It's within this smaller circle that our lives take on truly significant potential.

BELIEVE!

The first of the eight beHABITS! is beLIEVE! It reminds us of the importance of believing that we have a unique, creative contribution to make to the world. To our world. That and that alone must compel us to take care of our creative potential. We look for balance in life that will feed our ability to create rather than starve it. Why? Because we believe that our ability to create is something special—a treasure. And we need it. Your world needs it.

> *"Today you are You, that is truer than true.*
> *There is no one alive who is Youer than You."*
> Dr. Seuss

If I had stayed where I was the day I crashed and burned in October of 2007, this book would never have been written. More importantly, I would have lost the opportunity to love and encourage those who are most precious to me. People in my world would have lost those silly jokes that made them laugh, the words of encouragement that helped them take one more step in their journeys, and the art that inspired their own creative pursuits.

Your World Is Waiting

So, as we come to the end of our little journey together, what are you going to do? The demands on your time and talent are no less because you've read this book. The choices you have in front of you are the same ones you had before you ever heard of the beHABITS! What is different is…now you know. You know you have a choice. You can continue on a path that will ultimately burn you out. With that decision comes the loss of all that you could have contributed. On the other hand, you can acknowledge your ability to create as a gift and treat it accordingly. You see the world differently than anyone else. You have many unique, creative contributions to make to the world—to your world. And only you can make them.

Your world is waiting.

ABOUT THE AUTHOR

Jim Hough has been a creative professional for over 30 years. He's served as an illustrator, designer, writer, art director, creative director and in his current gig as vice president, executive creative director for a Midwest marketing communications firm. You can find more of his doodles, musings and fashion tips at www.BurnoutSucks.com.

To my readers:
I can't tell you how much I appreciate you taking the time to read this book. My prayer is that it will bless you in just the way you need it to. Please connect with me and let me know your thoughts:

eMail: jim@burnoutsucks.com

Twitter: @burnoutsucks

Facebook: https://www.facebook.com/jhoughbook

And be sure to sign up for the Burnout Sucks! Blog at:
www.BurnoutSucks.com

Acknowledgements:

Writing a book is hard. A lot harder than I thought it would be. And I would not have finished this project without the love and support of many people.

Anne Marie, my dear, sweet partner in life. You have been my soulmate, my rock, my comforter, my cheerleader, my editor, my sounding board, my reason for getting up at 4 a.m. to work on this thing. You are my one true love—the love of my life.

My dad, whose last words to me were, "I'm really proud of you. I love you." Thank you for teaching me to find the humor that sometimes hides in the dark corners of life.

My mom, who always wanted to write a book. Your unique, creative contribution to the world came in other forms. This one is for both of us.

Dan Miller, for the *Write to the Bank* workshop that showed me I could write a book. It's not the book I thought I was going to write, but your encouragement and teaching kept me moving forward.

Kent Julian, your *Live It Forward!* approach to life, the *Speak It Forward* workshop and Mastermind group (not to mention the *Write It Forward* workshop!) have all changed my life and given me, not just the tools to become an author and speaker, but the inspiration to put them to good use. I don't always speak for free, but when I do, it's not for free. ;0)

Andy Traub, your book, *The Early to Rise Experience*, transformed me from a lazy night owl into a productive morning person. Your contribution to this book, and to my ability to make my unique, creative contribution to the world, is immeasurable.

The Robert D, your book *20,000 Days and Counting* inspired my goal to get this thing launched before March 15, 2016, my 20,000th day.

The 48Days.net community, you are an amazing group of fellow travelers! Thank you for your encouragement, feedback and willingness to share your wealth of experience. I hope I can give back even a tiny fraction of what you have given to me.

Todd Henry, your book, *The Accidental Creative*, gave voice to the subject of being wildly creative and living to enjoy it. I'm sure that without your writing, speaking, blogging and podcasts, this book would never have been written.

Ron Bonger, your friendship, support and loyalty throughout the last 25 years and especially during the very darkest days of my burnout, quite literally saved my life. You are my brother forever.

Dr. Dennis E. Hensley, thank you for your editing and for making me a better writer.

My extended family and friends, including Dan, Diana, Tom, Sandy, Chris, Sid, Dad Hill, Terri, Sue, Eric, Laurie (SIL), and so many others, thank you for your encouragement and for always asking me, "How's the book coming?"

My heavenly Papa and Lord Jesus Christ. May this be a small part of glorifying You and enjoying You forever.

NOTES

Chapter 1. A Good Place to Start

1. Ford adopts the 40-hour work week: "Ford Motor Company Chronology". *The Henry Ford*. 2014. http://www.thehenry-ford.org/exhibits/fmc/chrono.asp
2. Greg McKeown, *Essentialism*, Crown Business, 2014
3. James Taylor, *Sun on the Moon*, from the album Never Die Young, Columbia/Legacy, 1988

Chapter 2. What Does Burnout Look Like?

1. "Elephant and the Blind Men". *Jainism Global Resource Center*. 2011 http://www.jainworld.com/education/stories25.asp
2. Statements taken from responses to an informal survey conducted by BurnoutSucks.com

Chapter 3. Down in Flames

1. Todd Henry, Accidental Creative, Penguin Group, 2011 The phrase "create-on-demand" was coined by Todd Henry and his organization, Accidental Creative, and is used with Todd's gracious permission.

Chapter 5. The beHABITS!

1. James A. Autry, *The Servant Leader,* Crown Business, 2004
2. "How long does it take to form a habit?" http://www.ucl.ac.uk/news/news-articles/0908/09080401
3. Andy Traub, *The Early to Rise Experience*, Take Permission Media Network; Revised edition, November 5, 2013
4. Ecclesiastes 1:9, New International Version of the Holy Bible, Zondervan

Chapter 6. beLEIVE!

1. *It's A Wonderful Life*. Dir. Frank Capra. Liberty Films. 1946. Film.

Chapter 7. beBRAVE!

1. Franklin D. Roosevelt. Presidential Inaugural Address. Washington, D.C. March 4, 1933. The text can be found at http://www.inaugural.senate.gov/swearing-in/address/address-by-franklin-d-roosevelt-1933

2. Karl Albrecht, Ph.D. "The (Only) 5 Fears We All Share. *Psychology Today*. March 22, 2012. ile://local-host/Karl Albrecht, Ph.D. http/::www.psychologytoday.com:blog:brainsnacks:201203:the-only-five-basic-fears-we-all-live

3. Seth Godin, *Poke the Box*, Do You Zoom, Inc., 2011

4. David Bayles and Ted Orland, *Art & Fear*, Image Continuum Press, April 1, 2001

5. Dr. James Dobson, *The New Hide or Seek*, Revell, a division of Baker Publishing Group, 1999

6. Steven Covey, *The 7 Habits of Highly Effective People*, Simon and Schuster; First edition, 1989

Chapter 9. bePLAYFUL!

1. Tanya Beatty. "Rubber band Babies". Online video clip. Youtube. June 12, 2013. Retrieved October 2013. https://www.youtube.com/watch?v=RDIoq1abDCY

2. "The Vision". The National Institute for Play. 2014. http://www.nifplay.org/http://www.mayoclinic.org/healthy-living/stress-management/in-depth/stress-relief/art-20044456

3. Mayo Clinic Staff. "Stress relief from laughter? It's no joke". Mayo Clinic. July 23, 2013. http://www.psychologytoday.com/blog/memory-medic/201307/does-humor-make-you-live-longer

4. Willian Klemm, Ph. D. "Does Humor Make You Live Longer?". *Psychology Today*. July 25, 2013. http://www.psychologytoday.com/blog/memory-medic/201307/does-humor-make-you-live-longer

Chapter 10. bePRESENT!

1. A poll conducted exclusively for FuzeBox by SurveyMonkey 2014 http://www.prnewswire.com/news-releases/fuzebox-survey-reveals-us-workforce-hampered-by-multitasking-and-disengagement-242217771.html
2. IBM Operating System/360 Concepts and Facilities - Witt, Bernard I. & Lambert, Ward
3. Wallis, Claudia (Mar 19, 2006). The Multitasking Generation. Retrieved 4/26/10.
4. *A Unified Attentional Bottleneck in the Human Brain*, 2011 http://www.pnas.org/content/108/33/13426.full.pdf
5. Chris Woolston, M.S. "Multitasking and Stress:. *HealthDaily*. March 11, 2015. http://consumer.healthday.com/encyclopedia/emotional-health-17/emotional-disorder-news-228/multitasking-and-stress-646052.html. As reported by Woolston, Gloria Mark and colleagues from the University of California at Irvine issued these findings at a conference for the Association for Computing Machinery
6. Todd Henry, *Accidental Creative*, Penguin Group, 2011
7. "Fade Out, Fade In". *M*A*S*H: Season Six*. 20th Century Fox Television, 2004. DVD
8. Steven Covey, *The 7 Habits of Highly Effective People*, Simon and Schuster; First edition, 1989
9. Julia Cameron, *The Artist's Way*, Penguin Group(USA), 1992

Chapter 11. beCONNECTED!

1. Jonathan Rauch. "Caring for Your Introvert". *The Atlantic Monthly*. March 2003. http://www.jonathanrauch.com/jrauch_articles/caring_for_your_introvert/
2. Coca-Cola Conversations. "I'd Like To Buy the World a Coke Commercial – 1971". Online video clip. *Youtube* https://www.youtube.com/watch?v=2msbfN81Gm0

3. "Robert Owen". *Wikipedia.* http://en.wikipedia.org/wiki/Robert_Owen.

Chapter 12. beRENEWED!
1. Jon Acuff, *Start: Punch Fear in the Face, Escape Average and Do Work That Matters*, Lampo Press, April 23, 2013
2. Detailed in Leanie Lerche Davis. "The Toll of Sleep Loss in America". *WebMD.* November 29, 2011. http://www.webmd.com/sleep-disorders/features/toll-of-sleep-loss-in-america

Chapter 13. beGRATEFUL!
1. Victor Frankl, *Man's Search for Meaning*, Pocket Books; Rev Updated edition, 1997

Chapter 14. Your World
1. Ranker Community. "The Most Influential People of All Time". *Ranker.* Accessed September 2014. http://www.ranker.com/crowdranked-list/the-most-influential-people-of-all-time
2. Steven Covey, *The 7 Habits of Highly Effective People*, Simon and Schuster; First edition, 1989

www.ingramcontent.com/pod-product-compliance
Lightning Source LLC
Chambersburg PA
CBHW060523030426
42337CB00015B/1983